A Manager's Guide to
Self-development

A Manager's Guide to Self-development

SIXTH EDITION

Mike Pedler, John Burgoyne, Tom Boydell

London   Boston   Burr Ridge, IL   Dubuque, IA   Madison, WI   New York   San Francisco   St. Louis   Bangkok
Bogotá   Caracas   Kuala Lumpur   Lisbon   Madrid   Mexico City
Milan   Montreal   New Delhi   Santiago   Seoul   Singapore   Sydney   Taipei   Toronto

McGraw-Hill Professional
McGraw-Hill Education
McGraw-Hill House
Shoppenhangers Road
Maidenhead
Berkshire
England
SL6 2QL

email: enquiries@openup.co.uk
world wide web: www.openup.co.uk

and Two Penn Plaza, New York, NY 10121–2289, USA
First published 2013

A catalogue record of this book is available from the British Library

ISBN-13: 978–0–07–714988–8 (pb)
ISBN-10: 0–07–714988–2 (pb)
eISBN: 978–0–07–715457–8

Library of Congress Cataloging-in-Publication Data
CIP data applied for

Typesetting and e-book compilations by
SR Nova Pvt Ltd., Bangalore, India

Fictitious names of companies, products, people, characters and/or data that may be used herein (in case studies or in examples) are not intended to represent any real individual, company, product or event.

Printed and bound in Great Britain by Bell & Bain Ltd, Glasgow

"Pedler, Burgoyne and Boydell have done it again. Their 6th Edition of *A Manager's Guide to Self Development* is engaging, innovative and exciting to use in anyone's self development. The exercises are fun and illuminating, and the pace is fast and energising. A must read for any manager wanting to be 'the best'."

Prof. Cary L. Cooper, CBE, Distinguished Professor of Organizational Psychology and Health,
Lancaster University Management School, UK

"I thoroughly recommend this sixth edition as a core self-development text for students and management practitioners at all levels. In lucid and readily accessible language it makes the key models of theory and practice available to all those who wish to take charge of their own learning. It is ideal for students of Business and Organisational Management at undergraduate and postgraduate levels and is equally suitable for both younger managers in the early parts of their career and experienced managers wishing to refresh their personal qualities after some years of operational experience. I read the first edition 35 years ago and have seen a generation of managers, trainers and consultants use it to develop successful careers. It is equally relevant in its new updated form for contemporary managers since it deals with fundamental principles of personal development. The trainers' guide is an especially welcome addition – as are the seven new activities."

Barry Curnow, Head of Human Resources & Organisational Behaviour Department,
University of Greenwich Business School, UK

"The book makes an unanswerable case for managers to engage in their own self development. Self managing – in learning and in life – is central to being effective in a whole range of work contexts. Sheep dip course continue to proliferate when the evidence is that self development in work is the key to success. This guide provides real support for managers to take charge of their own learning and all managers need to pay attention to making it happen."

Prof Ian Cunningham, Self Managed Learning College, Brighton, UK

"*A Manager's Guide to Self Development* has been a staple of the Personal Development module on the Executive MBA for some time. The mature framework and eclectic mix of self-study activities in the book complement the experiential and practical approach to Management Education at Henley. The changes introduced in the new edition mirror the strong focus on narrative and reflective sense-making, which are important in preparation for the positions of senior leadership our programme members aspire to."

Chris Dalton, Henley Business School, UK

"This book continues to be the shining light in guiding managers and leaders toward self-development. The sixth edition continues a grand tradition in the literature that Mike, John and Tom have provided from their very first edition. This is essential reading for managers from all organisations!"

Dr Gareth Edwards, Senior Lecturer in Organisation Studies, Bristol Business School,
University of the West of England, UK

"Fads and fashions in management development come and go but this is an ever-reliable source of inspiration. Even if organisations mistakenly believe they can cut back on developing their leaders and managers, this is a book that puts the power to act in the hands and heads of leaders and managers themselves. Welcome back, boys!"

Professor Jeff Gold, Leeds Business School, Leeds Metropolitan University, UK

"This book is an essential purchase for any manager who takes their development seriously. The practical activities engage the reader as an active learner: it will help managers improve their skills and experiment with better ways of working. This is a very timely and extended new edition that is highly recommended."

Kim Turnbull James, Professor of Executive Learning, Cranfield School of Management, UK

"It is with a great sense of privilege that I have been asked to comment on this book. My introduction to the book was in 1978 and it has become a staple resource for my teaching ever since. The authors all come from a tradition that recognises only too well that managers learn naturally, yet with the kind of structure, reflection and encouragement to take action whereby the learning process can be significantly enhanced.

The book also recognises the fact that developing individuals is inextricably linked to developing organisations and if individuals are to be effective they need to know themselves and develop appropriate skills and attitudes. The book sets out what these are and recognises that over time they change as organisations change, for example, as 'making contacts' has morphed into 'networking' and 'using power, mentorship and managing change' have crept into the lexicon. Where originally there were 39 activities related to management development there are now 57.

I fully endorse the sixth edition and will continue to use the ideas it contains with my own students."

Richard Thorpe, Professor of Management Development and Pro Dean Research,
Leeds University Business School, UK

Contents

Introduction

Chapter 1

The Philosophy of This Book

This book, which is an aid to management self-development rather than a repository of facts and theories, is based on a simple fundamental premise:

that any effective system for management development must increase the person's capacity and willingness to take control over, and responsibility for, events – particularly for themselves and their own learning.

While this is not a new concept, it is one that is not always recognized. The standard approach to training and development has been that of learning to get the right answer from authority figures – teachers, experts, bosses, parents – in other words, to do things 'properly'. In recent years, views have changed considerably. The emphasis has shifted from *training* to do things right, to *learning* to improve, to push out the frontiers of knowledge and performance – in other words, to do things better.

If asked to think about how we have learned, we may think first of what we have been taught. Yet less than 20% of significant learning comes in this way. Our research shows that if you ask people how they have learned the things that are really important to them, 80% comes from tackling the challenging situations in life. Moreover, in solving these problems we don't just deal with the immediate difficulty; we become better at solving problems in general. To a large extent, problem solving is learning.

Dealing with live problems is the fundamental managerial process, and it can also be the source of your significant learning – as long as you know how to learn from your experiences. When it comes to a 'crunch' decision such as selecting for a key appointment, what really matters is track record – whether the person has dealt successfully with difficult situations before. Completing formal management development programmes does not usually carry a lot of weight in these circumstances.

The implications are clear: to learn and to progress, first recognize the key management and leadership challenges, get into the action, reflect upon and learn from your experiences – and be seen to have done so.

Changing organizations

This new sixth edition of *A Manager's Guide to Self-development* sees many changes from the first edition of 35 years ago. While the title is as relevant as ever, our ideas about what makes for good management and leadership in organizations have evolved.

Leaders and managers today need to be more than ambitious in simple career terms. Success used to mean climbing higher and higher on the organizational climbing frame, with the occasional bold leap across to a higher level on an adjacent structure. But many of these climbing frames have collapsed in recent years: they have broken up, shrunk and become 'leaner' and 'flatter'. The grim experience for some managers has been of throwing each other off the frame to make room for the survivors, who get used to sideways moves and increased responsibilities. In this reality, just having a job becomes more prized, and sideways moves can offer variety and development opportunities.

There is now a realization that success and satisfaction do not necessarily come from 'possessing' a large chunk of managerial territory in an invulnerable blue chip company, but instead from being part of a well-run and effective network or organization that knows what it is doing, where it is going and what part each person's unique contribution can make. People prefer to work at what they believe is good and useful; and in organizations or networks which know why they are good and know how they can stay that way.

Working together to do better things

In good environments, everyone becomes more self-managing, aligning themselves with others through working to shared values and missions, rather than being directed by the external regulation of job descriptions and hierarchical supervision. Information technology also speeds this trend, distributing knowledge widely to make self-management more possible. Yet, at the same time, this is also the era of performance management where, driven by central targets, managers become local leaders, getting people enthused about learning to do things better – to improve themselves and their performance.

The downside of these performance and modernization efforts stems from their focus on easily measurable targets. These all too often result in the short term and the urgent pushing out the important and the long term. Simple targets can result in unhelpful competitions between individuals, teams and departments, and the 50% of us who are 'below average' get punished rather than rewarded for our efforts.

Many people now see the world as too complex to manage in these ways. Simple solutions may create worse problems elsewhere, and solving problems often means listening to the many and diverse stakeholders who want their voices to be heard. This requires managers to see the wider picture and appreciate the views of others who are 'different from us'. Organizational challenges cannot be tackled in isolation – they demand collaborative working with other individuals, teams, departments and agencies. 'Joined-up action' is essential, not only to do things better but to do better things together.

What is self-development?

It has yet to be shown that formal leadership and management development programmes have much impact on organizational performance. Why is this? One possibility is that they may, unintentionally, encourage people to be less self-reliant. These programmes teach leadership, finance, strategy and so on, but the message is in the medium. These underlying messages are:

There is an expert for every type of management problem; don't try to solve it on your own – call in the experts.

You don't know how to learn? Don't worry; you don't need to. We're here to manage that for you. If you need a 're-tread', don't try to do it yourself, come back to us.

Such messages deskill people. This book has a different message; in our view:

Self-development is personal development, with the person taking primary responsibility for their own learning and for choosing the means to achieve this. Ultimately, it is about increasing your capacity and willingness to take control over, and be responsible for, events.

Self-development can mean many things:

- developing specific qualities and skills
- improving your performance in your existing job
- advancing your career ... or
- achieving your full potential as a person.

This book is an invitation to work on these aspects of your own personal and professional development, and an opportunity to help with the development of other people around you and thereby make a wider contribution to doing better things. Good luck.

Chapter 2

How This Book Works

This book is in three parts. After this introduction, the second part helps you to diagnose your self-development needs in the context of your career and life, to set some learning goals for yourself and make a self-development plan to achieve them. Part 3 consists of 57 Activities or resources for you to use in achieving your goals and your plan. Part 4 is for trainers and contains ideas and methods for using this book in their work.

To progress your self-development, you first need to think about where you are now and where you want to be. What skills and qualities do you have now? What capabilities and aspects of yourself do you want to develop? Then you can work out your learning goals and plan your personal learning programme.

As you are likely to have limited time, this book is designed to be used a bit at a time, working on the Activities between meetings, in airports or on train journeys, and even in the bath. While some of the Activities need to be done at work, such as observing how meetings work and trying out different forms of action, others can be tackled in informal contacts, over lunch with colleagues, for instance, to test their perceptions against your own.

Planning for action and learning

Self-development is a continuous process. Review your progress and set new goals as time proceeds. When your target date arrives, evaluate your progress against your goals and decide what further action to take, if any. The learning cycle is shown in Fig. 2.1.

The ideal is to incorporate this way of thinking, diagnosing and goal setting into your everyday activities, thereby increasing your effectiveness on an on-going basis. The ideal is to incorporate this way of thinking, diagnosing and goal setting into your everyday life.

In Part 2 of this book:

Chapter 3, *A career/life-planning activity*, helps you to set your self-development plan in the wider context of how careers are constructed in large and small enterprises.

In Chapter 4, *The qualities of successful managers and leaders*, we introduce our research-based model that provides the basis and structure for this book.

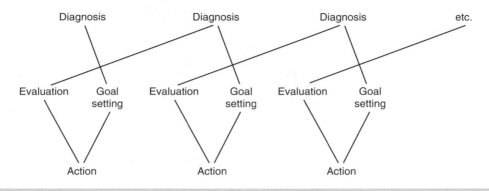

Figure 2.1   The learning cycle

Chapter 5, *Where to start? Assessing your learning priorities*, contains a questionnaire based on our model to help you to identify your abilities and needs and to set your priorities and goals for personal self-development.

As an aid to the achievement of your goals, Chapter 6, *How to select and use the activities*, provides a map to help you choose from the activities and other resources available in Part 3 of the book.

Part 3 consists of 57 activities for self-development. These are all designed to follow the learning cycle outlined above and can be done as part of your normal working life. Choose from these to move ahead with your personal managerial and leadership development.

PART 2

Planning Your Self-development

Chapter 3

A Career/Life-Planning Activity

This chapter offers you the opportunity to think about your managerial career in the context of your life as a whole. From this perspective, there are several issues that might affect you, for example:

- you may be wondering whether or not you want to become a manager at all?
- Or perhaps you are asking yourself whether you have what it takes to be a manager, in terms of your abilities and experiences?
- Alternatively, you may already be a manager and wondering if you have made the right choice ...
- or you may have been a manager for some time, and are now faced with questions such as: What is my next step?
- On the other hand, perhaps you are working for a large organization and wondering if you could start your own business?
- or perhaps you are becoming aware that your work/life balance is an increasing problem?
- or again perhaps you may have a feeling that something is missing. What is it that you *really* want from life?
- Finally, perhaps you are faced with a crisis such as redundancy, illness, separation. What does this mean for you?

These examples illustrate that it's not really possible to separate jobs and careers from the rest of our lives. To think about planning your career is also to think about the other aspects of your life as well.

If the idea of spending time planning your life seems a bit odd, consider this: *How many hours have you spent thinking about and planning:*

- your last holiday?
- selecting the house or apartment in which you live?

- buying your laptop, video camera, car, bicycle, or other favourite possession?
- your life?

Now rank these: first in order of the time you spent planning each, and then in order of importance.

If you do decide to spend some time planning your life and career, there are many life-planning exercises available. They differ in detail and also in the extent to what they focus on, with most concentrating mainly on the future. Here we offer you two ways to think about your career in the context of your life. You can do either or both of these:

- Method 1: *Career Biography* take an *inside-out* approach focusing on your career over time, from the past to the present and how you would like it to be in the future.
- Method 2: *Contextual Intelligence* helps you to consider your career from the *outside in*, in the light of the contexts – personal, organizational and global – that you are working in.

N.B. To do justice to both Methods 1 & 2 might take you at least three hours – which is why we suggest doing a step at a time. However, if you want to go faster, a 'lite' version is included at the end of the chapter. However, faster is not always better.

Method 1: Your career biography

This takes the form of a series of tasks and questions to give you insights into your career biography, by looking at your:

- *past*: the events, periods and themes and achievements in your life so far
- *present*: the current issues and questions in your life
- *future*: choosing the priorities and choices from alternative courses of action.

To do this properly might take some time; you can do it perhaps over a few days, tackling a step or two at a time. It's a very good idea to work on it with a partner or a small group, sharing with each other after each step.

THE PAST

Step 1: Events

Think back and write down 10 or 12 key events, incidents or turning points in your life to date. (Start from the present and work backwards.)

A key event is something that has a special significance and sticks in your memory, and which perhaps marked a turning point of some kind. Some events will be things that happened quickly, but others may have lasted much longer – for weeks or even months.

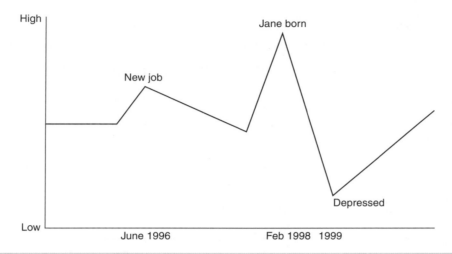

Figure 3.1   *Lifeline graph*

Step 2: Life-line

Now take a sheet of paper and draw a 'graph' of these events in your life, with time along the horizontal axis, and feelings up the side. So, when you were feeling good, you would have a peak; and when you were feeling bad, there would be a trough (see Figure 3.1).

SHARING: If you are working with a partner or in a group, now share your events and life-line. Talk to each other about what happened. How did you feel? What did you do? You could do all this on your own, pausing to reflect and talk to yourself.

Step 3: Periods

Look over your life-line of events. Now working forwards this time, starting from the earliest, look at the *periods* between events. Give each of these a label or title to describe how they were, what they felt like, and so on. Some people use song titles for this, the titles of books – whatever works for you. Write these titles of periods on your life-line.

Step 4: Themes

Now looking over the picture that is emerging of your life from your list of events and periods, what *themes* can you see emerging? For example:

- underlying patterns of thoughts, feelings or behaviours that appear at regular intervals, or in certain circumstances;
- aspects or characteristics that seem to be there for you all the time, or that appear inter-mittently from time to time.

SHARING: This is another useful time to share with a partner or group. By now you may be able to see themes in each other's biographies.

Step 5: Achievements

Now list up to 10 achievements in your life to date, using the following categories:

(a) Your FAMILY, FRIENDS, and OTHER PERSONAL RELATIONSHIPS

_____

_____

_____

_____

(b) Your CAREER

_____

_____

_____

_____

(c) Your MATERIAL WEALTH and POSSESSIONS

_____

_____

_____

_____

(d) Your HEALTH, PERSONAL DEVELOPMENT and LEARNING

_____

_____

_____

_____

(e) Your SPIRITUAL/ARTISTIC DEVELOPMENT

_____

_____

_____

_____

What do you think of these lists? How do they make you feel? (If you are working with a partner, *share* your lists and your feelings.)

THE PRESENT

Step 6: Questions and issues coming your way

Now move into the present by looking at questions and issues emanating from the work you have done to date. The following are three ways to identify these questions. (As before, this may be easier working with a partner.)

1. *The overall picture of your life so far.*
    If this was someone else's biography, how would you react to it? What unfinished business or next tasks do you see for that person? What decisions need to be faced?
    But, of course, this is your biography, and these are *your* issues. Write them down here:

    _____

    _____

    _____

    _____

2. *Themes.*
    Now look at your themes that have always been there, have appeared from time to time or are newly emerging. These can often give a good indication of the questions and issues coming your way. Write down any of these which you think are unfinished for you:

    _____

    _____

    _____

    _____

3. *People in your consciousness.*
    We all carry around in our consciousness a 'network' of people that we interact with in our lives – family members, friends, colleagues, and so on. Some may be people we haven't seen for a long time, but who still influence us and are in our 'consciousness net', perhaps saying things or asking us questions. Think of all these people, both close and more distant, and write down what they are saying to you, or asking you:

    _____

    _____

    _____

    _____

THE FUTURE

Step 7: Future achievements

You have drawn up a list of past achievements – but what about things that you have not yet achieved? Here are three ideas for generating some ideas about this:

(a) Write your own obituary, as you would like it to appear in a newspaper of your choice:

_____

_____

_____

_____

(b) Imagine a perfect day some time in the future; including all those things that you would like for yourself. What are you doing? How does it feel? Who else is there?

_____

_____

_____

_____

(c) What are the unrealized goals you have with respect to the following:

Your CAREER?

_____

_____

_____

_____

Your FAMILY, FRIENDS and OTHER PERSONAL RELATIONSHIPS?

_____

_____

_____

_____

Your MATERIAL WEALTH and POSSESSIONS?

_____

_____

_____

_____

Your HEALTH, PERSONAL DEVELOPMENT and LEARNING?

_____

_____

_____

_____

Your SPIRITUAL/ARTISTIC DEVELOPMENT?

_____

_____

_____

_____

OTHER GOALS

Step 8: Intentions

By now, you will have a lot of data about yourself, your biography, and the questions coming your way, together with the goals you still want to achieve. It's now time to choose your priorities.

Look over all your data and select up to five issues and goals as your priorities. For each of these, write down your intentions – what you would like to achieve for each of your priorities:

1.

2.

3.

4.

5.

Step 9: Options for action

Next think about the actions you can take to achieve your intentions. In most situations there will always be several possible courses of action, each with its pros and cons. An old rule is that there are always four alternatives in any situation, namely:

- *change the situation*: do something about it, be proactive;
- *change yourself*: examine your own attitudes and behaviour, and change something about you;
- *change your relationship with the situation*: come to terms with it in some way, decide to live with it;
- *leave the situation*: find a constructive way to move on.

Look at the five priorities you chose in Step 8 above, and for each of them choose an option for action:

1.

2.

3.

4.

5.

Here again, working with a partner or in a small group can be extremely useful, as you can share and help each other to generate alternatives. You can also think together over the relative advantages and disadvantages of each alternative, thus enabling you to *choose* one particular course of action.

Force Field Analysis is a useful technique to help with this sort of choice; you can find a worked example in Activity 16 later in this book.

Step 10: First steps

Finally, you are now approaching implementing your chosen course of action. So think about your first steps:

- When are you going to start?
- What will you actually do? How?

Write brief notes on dates and planned actions against the five priorities in Step 9.

KEEPING GOING: You now have a plan. Good luck with that. Make sure you review progress from time to time, revising your plans, taking account of changes and new issues and keep going.

Method 2: Contextual intelligence

Method 2 helps you to consider your career in the light of questions such as these:

■ Why do some people succeed whereas others, equally or more talented, do less well?

■ Why is a person's track record in one organization not always a good guide to their future performance in a different setting?

This alternative way of thinking about your career focuses on what is going on around you. This 'outside-in' approach aims to sharpen your contextual intelligence and help make you a first-class 'noticer'.

This is *not* about engaging in a complex and detailed analysis to obtain right answers, but about taking a quick scan of the horizon – what's out there that I should be taking into account?

Step 1: Picturing the context

Choose a current career challenge on which to focus: what is it that you really want to do? What is stopping you? Pick a particular challenge that you are facing, and test your ideas for action by questioning them with all the contextual intelligence you can muster.

A context can be thought of as having several layers or rings, from local to global. Starting from our own local life context, we can extend the gaze to social, community and organizational settings, and then still wider to the global society and epoch in which we live.

■ PERSONAL: Your life context

■ ORGANIZATIONAL & COMMUNITY context

■ GLOBAL (Era): historical, economic, social, political, technological, cultural, ecological and environmental contexts.

Start with a large sheet of paper (A3 or flip chart size) or perhaps a whiteboard, or the computer equivalent. As in Method 1 it will be very helpful to do this with a partner or small group of other interested people.

Over the next three steps you will be drawing (and writing in) three concentric circles, so draw three pictures as a series of widening circles or concentric rings as in the illustrations below; start with the PERSONAL and work outwards to the GLOBAL.

For each of the three layers, we have provided eight contextual factors that might affect the challenge you have in mind. Add your own thoughts on the issues and how important they are. If you are working in a group, you could divide into three at this point and each take one aspect of the context to work on and to bring back to the whole group.

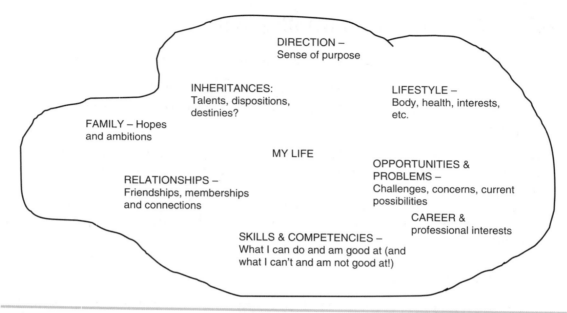

*Figure 3.2   **PERSONAL** context*

Step 2: PERSONAL context: Your life

First, think about your PERSONAL context. Think about the important aspects of your life that influence what you do.

Draw your own picture like the example in Figure 3.2 to assemble these important qualities, relationships, aspirations and possibilities. Make sure you include the things that are most important to you.

N.B. As there are two further contextual layers to come, remember to put your first picture in the middle of the page or whiteboard with plenty of space around it.

Now ask yourself three questions about each of these important areas of your life:

■ What am I trying to do with this aspect of my life?

■ What's getting in the way of what I want at this time?

■ What are the opportunities here to do something about this?

Make some notes about your answers. You can either write on your picture or make a list as in Table 3.1.

Table 3.1 Notes about my PERSONAL context

PERSONAL CONTEXT	NOTES	IMPACT (high/medium/low)
INHERITANCES – Talents, dispositions, destinies?		
SKILLS & COMPETENCIES		
FAMILY – Hopes & ambitions		
RELATIONSHIPS – Friendships, memberships & connections		
CAREER & professional interests		
DIRECTION – Sense of purpose		
LIFESTYLE – Body, health, interests, etc.		
OPPORTUNITIES & PROBLEMS – Challenges, concerns, current possibilities		
? (Add your own)		
? (Add your own)		

Step 3: ORGANIZATIONAL & COMMUNITY context

Now, think about the organizations and communities in which you live and work – residential and professional. How do these influence what you can do? And what are the opportunities here to extend your influence?

Draw another layer to the picture you drew in Figure 3.2 to assemble these important qualities, relationships, aspirations and possibilities (Figure 3.3). Make sure you include the things that are most important to you.

Ask yourself the following three questions about each of the important areas of your ORGANIZATIONAL & COMMUNITY context:

■ How are we (i.e. the organizations or community) doing in this aspect of our corporate/community life?

■ What are the prospects and likely future events in this area?

■ How does this aspect affect what I/we want to do next?

Make some notes about your answers. Either put notes on picture or make a list as in Table 3.2.

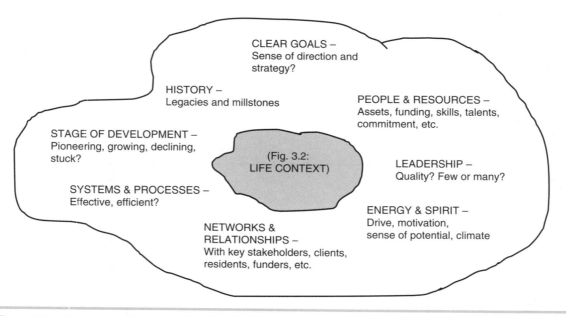

Figure 3.3 *ORGANIZATIONAL & COMMUNITY context*

Table 3.2   Notes about my ORGANIZATIONAL & COMMUNITY context

ORGANIZATIONAL & COMMUNITY context	NOTES	IMPACT (high/medium/low)
CLEAR GOALS – Sense of direction & strategy?		
HISTORY – Legacies & millstones		
PEOPLE & RESOURCES – Assets, funding, skills, talents, commitment, etc.		
LEADERSHIP – Quality? Few or many?		
NETWORKS & RELATIONSHIPS – With key stakeholders, clients, residents, funders, etc.		
SYSTEMS & PROCESSES – Effective, efficient?		
ENERGY & SPIRIT – Drive, motivation, sense of potential, climate		
STAGE OF DEVELOPMENT – Pioneering, growing, declining, stuck?		
? (Add your own)		
? (Add your own)		

Step 4: The GLOBAL context

Now, think more widely about the world and the era we are in. What are the national, international, global and environmental influences that impact on your world?

Draw a third layer to the picture as in Figure 3.2, and consider some of the wider forces that are having an impact on what you want to do – in your life, in your organization and in the communities to which you belong (Figure 3.4).

Ask yourself the following three questions about each of the important areas of your GLOBAL context:

■ What's coming up in this area that bears upon the current challenge?

■ What is there here that could help us adapt our response to this challenge?

■ What do we need to know more about?

Make some notes about your answers. Either put notes on the picture or make a list as in Table 3.3.

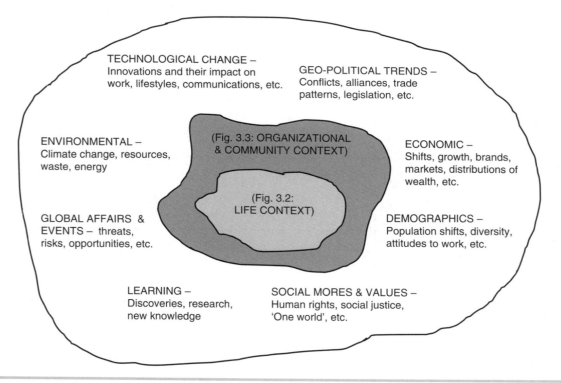

Figure 3.4   GLOBAL context

Table 3.3 Notes about the GLOBAL context

GLOBAL CONTEXT	NOTES	IMPACT (high/medium/low)
GEO-POLITICAL TRENDS – Conflicts, alliances, trade patterns, legislation, etc.		
ECONOMIC – Shifts, growth, brands, markets, distributions of wealth, etc.		
TECHNOLOGICAL CHANGE – Innovations and their impact on work, lifestyles, communications, etc.		
ENVIRONMENTAL – Climate change, resources, waste, energy		
GLOBAL AFFAIRS & EVENTS – threats, risks, opportunities, etc.		
LEARNING – Discoveries, research, new knowledge		
SOCIAL MORES & VALUES – Human rights, social justice, 'One world', etc.		
DEMOGRAPHICS – Population shifts, diversity, attitudes to work, etc.		
? (Add your own)		
? (Add your own)		

Lite version

We recommend doing both Methods 1 and 2 of this career/life-planning activity, but if you are really pressed for time, this 'lite' version will start you thinking about the issues covered in more detail above (Table 3.4).

This is a simple five question meditation – start with where you are now, then look at how you got here; then proceed to where you want and expect to go, and finish with the implications for your development.

As you do this, scan back through the earlier parts of the chapter to pick up ideas as they strike you to enrich your thinking and planning below.

Table 3.4 **My CAREER: Lite version**

CAREER/LIFE QUESTIONS	My NOTES on these questions
1. How have I got where I am today?	
2. Where am I now exactly?	
3. Where do I expect and want to go in the future?	
4. What contextual factors are most likely to impact my career and life?	
5. What are the implications for what I need to do and learn to help make this happen?	

Conclusion

Exploring your ideas in this way will help to broaden your perspective on life and the way in which you think about your career. The career biography approach focuses on you – your past, present and possible futures. In contrast, the outside-in contextual intelligence approach helps you notice what is going on around you. There are a great variety of possible contexts, and planning your life and career well demands a shrewd understanding both of yourself and of all the contexts in which you live and work.

The Qualities of Successful Managers and Leaders

This book is a programme for self-development based on the qualities of the effective manager or leader. Before going on to outline these qualities, and explain why we think they contribute to successful managing, pause for a moment and jot down your own views.

■ What do you think leadership and management *is*? What are the main features of this kind of work?

■ What are the main qualities required to be a successful manager and leader?

Our framework of *The 11 Qualities of the Effective Manager* is based on a research project and also from our own experience of managerial and leadership work. The research project identified the qualities that were found more often in successful managers than in those judged to be less successful. Successful managers were those who had risen to a senior post, who were significantly younger on average for their level of seniority ('fast trackers') or, most importantly, managers of any age or level who were seen as doing their jobs with above average effectiveness.[1]

The research identified 10 attributes that were more often possessed by the successful managers, to which we have added another one. These *11 Qualities of the Effective Manager* form the basis for the self-development programme provided in this book:

1. Situational facts
2. Professional knowledge and skills
3. Sensitivity to events
4. Analytical skills
5. People skills
6. Emotional resilience
7. Initiative
8. Creativity
9. Mental agility
10. Ability to learn
11. Self-knowledge

The 11 Qualities of the Effective Manager fall into three groups, which are also three different levels. Qualities 1 and 2 are the foundation level: they represent two kinds of basic knowledge and information that any leader or manager needs for making decisions and taking action.

The second level of Qualities 3–7 consists of the specific skills and attributes that directly affect behaviour and performance. Quality 3 – *Sensitivity to events* – is the means by which people acquire the basic knowledge and information involved at the foundation level of Qualities 1 and 2.

Qualities 8–11 form the third or 'meta' level. These are the abilities that enable people to develop and deploy the second-level skills and capacities of Qualities 3–7. They are called 'meta-qualities' because they help people to develop the situation-specific skills needed in particular contexts (see Figure 4.1).

Many of these 11 Qualities are interconnected – that is, possession of one contributes to possession of another. There follows a short explanation of each of them.

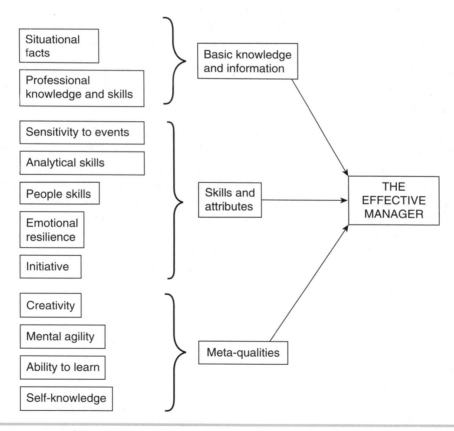

FIGURE 4.1   *The 11 Qualities of the Effective Manager*

Basic knowledge and information

1. *Situational facts.*

Successful managers and leaders know what's what in and around their organizations. You need to have a command of such basic facts as goals and plans (both long and short term), product knowledge, the roles and who's who in the organization and industry, the relationships between various units, your own job and what's expected of you. These days relevant information includes global knowledge of trends, markets and local conditions everywhere. If you don't store all this information, then you need to know where to get it when you need it. This increasingly involves the Internet and all kinds of IT-based resources, as well as four personal networks of contacts.

2. *Professional knowledge and skills.*

This includes all 'technical' and specialist knowledge, such as information technology, marketing techniques, engineering knowledge, relevant legislative, financial and human resourcing expertise. These are required not because you need them to act as a technical professional, but because you need to know about them to make managerial and leadership decisions. For example, you might need to know what information should be handed on between shifts in a factory, or as the leader of an operating theatre you need to know enough about the operation to help plan staff, resources and time.

Skills and attributes

3. *Sensitivity to events.*

People vary in the degree to which they can sense what is happening in a particular situation. To be a successful manager, you need to be sensitive to events and be able to tune in to what's going on. You need to be perceptive and open to information – 'hard' information, such as facts and figures, and 'soft' information, such as the feelings of other people. If you have this kind of sensitivity, you are able to respond in appropriate ways to situations as they arise. This sensitivity needs to be both 'local' (what is happening around you) and 'global (what is happening on a world scale). All kinds of technical and human information-getting skills are relevant here, as is having a network of informants.

4. *Analytical skills.*

As a manager or leader, you are very much concerned with making decisions. Decisions can sometimes be made logically, using appropriate techniques, but they often require the ability to weigh the pros and cons in uncertain or ambiguous situations. This calls for a high level of judgement and even intuition. You must therefore develop judgement skills, including the ability to cope with ambiguity and uncertainty; and learn to strike a balance between objective logic and the need at times to be guided by subjective feelings. This requires the ability to be critical both in terms of being able to question otherwise taken-for-granted

assumptions and also to concentrate on what makes the biggest difference to important outcomes.

5. *People skills.*

One old definition of managing and leading is 'getting things done through other people', and while this is incomplete today, it does point to the key attribute of interpersonal skills. Any successful leader or manager develops a range of interpersonal and social skills: communicating, coaching, negotiating, persuading, selling, networking, resolving conflicts and working with authority and power. As before, this is both local, being aware of the thoughts and feelings of people in your team, and global, the feeling on the streets in any global hotspot.

6. *Emotional resilience.*

All responsible jobs involve emotional stress and strain. This is a natural consequence of working in demanding situations, meeting targets and deadlines, and dealing with dilemmas, decisions and conflicts, within a context of uncertainty and ambiguity.

To be successful, you have to be resilient to cope. Being 'resilient' means not only that you are able to keep going but also that when stressed you don't become thick-skinned and insensitive, and cope by maintaining self-control and by 'giving' or bending to some extent. 'Emotional intelligence' may be relevant here, though it is not quite the same thing. The same can be said about the current fashion for coaching, though this is supposed to be just that and not therapy.

7. *Initiative.*

To be an effective leader or manager, you need to work towards a purpose or goal, and not merely respond to demands, although this may be the right thing to do on some occasions. At times, one has to respond to the needs of the immediate situation. Whereas a successful manager considers also the longer term, a less successful manager responds to the immediate pressure in a relatively unthinking or uncritical way. Taking initiative also includes seeing the job through, being dedicated and committed, having a sense of mission, and taking responsibility for things that happen rather than passing the buck to someone else.

Meta-qualities

8. *Creativity.*

By creativity we mean the ability to come up with unique responses to situations, and to have the insight to recognize and adopt useful new approaches. Creativity is not just about having new ideas oneself, but also having the ability to recognize and encourage the good ideas of other people. Creativity is often defined as having a new idea, and innovation as driving this through to a new product or service. We mean creativity that at least has the potential for this, perhaps in combination with 'initiative'.

9. *Mental agility.*

Although related to general intelligence, the concept of mental agility includes the ability to grasp problems quickly, to think of several things at once, to switch rapidly from one problem

or situation to another, to see quickly the whole situation (rather than ponderously ploughing through all its components), and to 'think on one's feet'. Given the hectic and ever-changing nature of organizational life, mental agility is an essential quality for success.

10. *Ability to learn.*

The importance of the skills of learning is one of the more interesting discoveries of research on managerial and leadership work. Data from observing and interviewing managers shows that a significant proportion of your success will rely on the presence or absence of habits and skills of learning:

- Good learners *use a range of different learning processes*, from receiving formal and informal inputs from training courses or coaching to reflection – the personal process of analysing and reorganizing their experiences and ideas – which can lead to discovery learning, or the generating of personal meaning from one's own experiences.

- Successful people *are more independent as learners*; they take responsibility for the 'rightness' of what is learned, rather than depending passively and uncritically on authority figures such as teachers or other experts to define 'the truth'. However, good managers do not reinvent the wheel, and know where to go to find the information they need.

- Successful managers *are capable of abstract as well as practical thinking*; they can relate and connect concrete ideas to abstract ones (and vice versa). This ability, sometimes known as a 'helicopter mind', enables people to generate their own theories from practice, and to develop their own practical ideas from theory.

- Effective managers and leaders are more likely to have *a wider view of the nature of the skills involved* in their work. For example, they are more likely to recognize the range of abilities as presented in this model of *The 11 Qualities of the Effective Manager*, than to see their work as a unitary activity, involving, for example, simply dealing with staff or making decisions.

11. *Self-knowledge.*

What each of us does is affected not only by the way we see our job or role, but also by our goals, values, feelings, strengths, weaknesses and a host of other personal factors. To maintain their self-command, successful leaders and managers must be aware of these self-attributes and the part they play in influencing their actions. The successful manager therefore needs the skills of introspection, and to be able to do something with the outcome of this. Being aware of one's own strengths and weaknesses in terms of a list like this is part of it.

Qualities or competencies?

In recent years, the idea of competencies has become very popular in the training and development world, and considerable efforts go into identifying competencies for a range of jobs, including those of managers and leaders.

We prefer the word 'qualities' for the reasons listed below. But whatever the term used, while it is useful to have frameworks to give people an idea of the kinds of knowledge, skills, abilities, and so on that may be appropriate in a given job, it is misleading to use any such framework rigidly. The person doing the job should be the final judge of what is useful in performing it effectively. We offer *The 11 Qualities of the Effective Manager* as a guide, not as a right answer – take it or leave it, take some of it, modify it, add to it, it's up to you.

No one is against competence, a wholly admirable thing to give or to receive. The dangers appear, especially in the sort of discretionary work that most leaders and managers do, when *single, external measures* are used to define competence and, by implication, incompetence. We hold that all skills and abilities are *personal qualities*, learned, exercised and owned by individual people. The provider and the receiver of a service may define competence, incompetence or excellence in a way that does not make sense outside that context.

Finally, while we are keen to help you become more competent, we are also interested in performance that goes well beyond the meaning of competent. For people whose standards of work are well beyond the norm, the word 'competent' is faint praise. Such people – and they are found in every field – are creative artists in what they do, their work a personal expression of inner aspiration and outer expectation.

Summary: so what?

Everything written in this book is our opinion. To use it as an aid to your self-development, you must decide how much you share these views, and what they mean, personally, to you.

Having read this chapter, why not write down your reactions to it? How do you feel about it? Interested? Bored? Sceptical? Enthusiastic?

Activity 8 (in Part 3) involves keeping a personal journal to keep a note of your experiences in order to learn from them. If reading these first chapters has been a useful experience so far, you will enhance and consolidate your learning by working through Activity 8 now, before proceeding further.

Reference

1. Burgoyne JG and Stuart R. The nature, use and acquisition of managerial skills and other attributes, *Personal Review* 5(4), 1976, pp. 19–29.

Chapter 5

Where to Start? Assessing Your Learning Priorities

In the previous chapter we introduced *The 11 Qualities of the Effective Manager*, which provide the model and structure for the Activities that form the third part of this book.

One way of approaching the Activities is to work through them in their order of appearance, but a much better way is to determine your own priorities and choose Activities based on these. This chapter offers three alternative ways to set your priorities and goals for self-development. These are as follows:

1. Reflective introspection
2. Conversation with a partner
3. Self-administered questionnaire

Different people like different methods and you may find one of these more attractive than the others, as they appeal to different learning styles and preferences. Of course, you can use more than one method and compare the results.

This chapter also contains a simple process for setting your development goals that can be applied whatever the method you choose.

Deficiency or abundance?

Many approaches to setting priorities for learning take a 'deficiency' approach – focusing on gaps or weaknesses in a person's abilities and 'diagnosing' what's wrong. In recent years, an *Appreciative Inquiry* approach has emerged, which offers an alternative perspective that informs the methods here. This involves identifying strengths as well as deficits, so that you can choose to enhance your strengths, as well as seeking to improve on weaknesses.

Method 1: Reflective introspection

There is an old saying that talking to yourself is the first sign of madness; but it is also a way of having a conversation with yourself or coaching yourself.

This method involves you thinking about each of the *11 Qualities* in some depth. This will suit the more reflective person, or you might choose this precisely because you want to practise these reflective skills.

To help you work through the *11 Qualities*, Table 5.1 offers key questions for you to consider.

First, study the outline descriptions of *The 11 Qualities of the Successful Manager* in Chapter 4. Second, decide whether you wish to make your own notes or would prefer to score your responses as you go. If you wish to score yourself, there are two columns to the right where you can do this:

- *Performance* column – use a 3- or 5-point scale to rate what you consider is your current performance on this Quality, where 1 = 'not good at this' and 3 (or 5) = 'very good at this'. We suggest that you score for the whole Quality, not each individual question.

- *Importance* column – here you can set your priorities with the performance scores as a guide.

Table 5.1 Qualitative questions for use in conversations with yourself and/or with a partner

The 11 Qualities of the Successful Manager		QUESTIONS	SCORES	
			Performance	Importance

1	Situational facts	• How much do you know about what's going on in and around your organization or network?
		• What are your sources of information?
		• How extensive are your contacts?
		• How many people do you know in and around your organization or network? This might include people senior or more junior to you, managers and other staff in your own team or elsewhere, such as customers, neighbours and competitors.
		• How many have you ever spoken with?
		• What do you know about
		  ○ what they do – their role, their purpose?
		  ○ their challenges?
		  ○ how they see your organization or network?
		  ○ what they are trying to achieve – their aspirations?		

Table 5.1 (*continued*)

The 11 Qualities of the Successful Manager		QUESTIONS	SCORES	
			Performance	Importance
		• How much do you know about policies, plans and strategies that might affect you, directly or indirectly? • What do you know about external trends – social, legal, political, market, technical, international – that may have an effect on your organization or network? • Can you think of some recent occasions when you were thankful that you knew some important information? • Conversely, can you think of some occasions when you wished you had more information? • What do you do to keep up to date on all these things?		
2	Professional knowledge and skills	• How would you describe, define or label your job or role in technical or professional terms? • What do you do to keep up to date with new ideas, techniques and approaches in your area of professional specialization? • How much time do you spend reading specialist journals? • How much time do you spend browsing the web in relation to your area of professional specialization? • How do you get guidance on technical, specialist or professional aspects of your job (e.g. engineer, health professional, accountant, social worker, lawyer, HR specialist, scientist, film maker, farmer)?		
3	Sensitivity to events	• What do you do to make sure that you are tuned in to what's happening in a given situation? In your own immediate sphere of influence? In your organization or network in general? In the broader external context – social, political, economic, environmental? • How aware are you of your own thoughts, thinking processes, assumptions? • How confident are you that your thoughts and assumptions are correct?		

(continued)

Table 5.1 (continued)

The 11 Qualities of the Successful Manager		QUESTIONS	SCORES	
			Performance	Importance
		• How aware are you of what other people are thinking (colleagues, subordinates, boss, external stakeholders such as customers, suppliers, neighbours, competitors)? What assumptions are they making? How do these compare with yours? • How aware are you of how such other people are feeling? • How aware are you of what such other people want to do? Are in fact doing? What they want you to do? • What sort of situations or 'happenings' do you find particularly difficult to weigh up and make sense of? • How aware are you of external influences on your organization or network – social, political and economic events and their effects?		
4	Analytical skills	• What do you find most difficult about making decisions? • Are there any types of decisions, or situations in which decisions are called for, that you find particularly difficult? • How do you feel about having to make judgements when ideally you would like more information? • Can you identify some 'good' decisions that you have made? What was there about them that makes you think they were 'good' decisions? What did you do to achieve this success? • Conversely, can you identify some 'bad' decisions (perhaps including some times when you couldn't make a decision at all)? Why do you think they were 'bad' decisions? What would you have liked to have done differently?		
5	People skills	• Can you think of occasions when you did a good job of handling 'the people aspects' – using people skills? Why do you think you handled them well? What did you do that led to this achievement?		

Table 5.1 (*continued*)

The 11 Qualities of the Successful Manager		QUESTIONS	SCORES	
			Performance	Importance
		• Conversely, can you think of occasions when on reflection you would have liked to have handled people and used your people skills better? What might you have done differently to achieve a better result? • How do you handle situations involving interpersonal conflict? • What do you do to try to ensure that people understand you when you communicate with them? • What do you do to try to ensure that you understand other people when they communicate with you? • What do you do to identify and understand what other people think about you? How they feel about you? • Can you think of occasions when you think you did a good job of working collaboratively with others? With your immediate colleagues? With people from other departments, professions, organizations or networks? What makes you think that you did a good job? What did you do that contributed to this achievement? • Conversely, can you think of occasions when what might have been a good collaborative activity or venture in fact failed? What makes you think this way? What did you do – or didn't do – that contributed to this disappointment?		
6	Emotional resilience	• How do you cope with feelings of stress, tension, anxiety or fatigue? • With whom do you talk about your worries and anxieties? • Can you think of occasions when you think you did a good job of handling a stressful situation? What makes you believe that you handled them well? What did you do that led to this achievement? • Conversely, can you think of occasions when you wish you had handled a stressful situation better? What makes you think that you could have handled them better? What might you have done differently to achieve a better result? • What do you do when you become emotional?		

(continued)

Table 5.1 (*continued*)

The 11 Qualities of the Successful Manager		QUESTIONS	SCORES	
			Performance	Importance
7	Initiative	• Can you think of times when you took the lead in a difficult or uncertain situation? What enabled you to do so? To what extent is this typical of the way you behave? • Conversely, can you think of times when you waited for someone else to take the lead when things were difficult or uncertain? Why was this? To what extent is this typical of the way you behave? • Can you think of times when you felt that you were in control of your own behaviour? What makes you believe that? What did you do that led to this positive feeling? • Conversely, can you think of times when you felt that you were not in control, but driven by others or situational pressures? What might you have done to take control yourself? What stopped you from doing so? • Can you see any pattern of situations where you tend to be independent and proactive, rather than dependent and reactive?		
8	Creativity	• What would you say are the most original, unusual or creative decisions or actions you have taken in the past 12 months – at work or outside? • What were the circumstances that enabled you to be creative like that? Can you see any pattern in this? • Can you think of times when you would like to have been more creative but were not able to be so? Why was that? Again can you see any patterns here? • How do you respond when other people suggest new, unusual or creative ways of doing things?		
9	Mental agility	• How good are you at handling several challenges, problems or tasks at the same time? • How often do you get what might be seen as 'sudden flashes of insight'? Can you think of any examples?		

Table 5.1 (*continued*)

The 11 Qualities of the Successful Manager		QUESTIONS	SCORES	
			Performance	Importance
		• How comfortable are you at handling what appear to be contradictory ideas or pieces of information? Can you think of examples of situations when you did this pretty well? Or not as well as you would have liked? • Can you think of some occasions that required you to think quickly, on your feet as it were? How did you handle these? What happened as a result?		
10	Ability to learn	• How good are you at learning – facts, ideas, procedures, skills – from other authorities such as trainers, experts, books, manuals? Can you think of times when you did these well, and times when you wished you had done better? Why was this? • To what extent are you able to reflect on experiences and learn from them – creating your own ideas or ways of doing things? Can you think of examples when you were successful in this way? Or when you wished you had been able to do better? • What about learning to achieve things with others? Your immediate colleagues? People from other teams, professions, organizations or networks?		
11	Self-knowledge	• How well do you think you know yourself? • How would you describe yourself? • To what extent are you aware of your feelings and the effect they are having on your behaviour? • Can you identify times when understanding what you were thinking, and/or how you were feeling, and/or what you wanted to do, affected your behaviour? • Conversely, can you identify any times when not being able to understand what you were thinking, feeling or wanting to do affected your behaviour? • What picture do you have of what you'll be doing – or would like to be doing – next year? In 3 years? In 10 years?		

Take your time to work through the questions. This is not a questionnaire designed for speedy completion, but instead a thoughtful survey guide and a simple 'ready reckoner' of your abilities on *The 11 Qualities of the Successful Manager*.

When you have worked through Table 5.1, look back over your answers. Do any of the *11 Qualities* call out in particular for further development, either because you are lacking in them or because they are strengths that you want to improve on further?

If you can't easily arrive at priorities for development, try the following: write each of the *11 Qualities* on a card so that you can shuffle them. Pick two at random from the pack and then choose between them: which is your first priority for development? Then choose another at random, and locate it relative to the first two – before the first, between the two or after the second? Proceed in turn with all the cards, until you have ranked the *11 Qualities* in order of their developmental priority for you.

When you have your priorities, use Table 5.2 to note your development goals, perhaps linking these with the 57 Activities in Part 3 of this book (the guidance system for this can be found in Table 6.1 in the following chapter).

Table 5.2 **My development goals**

PRIORITY ORDER of *The 11 Qualities of the Successful Manager*	ACTIVITIES from PART 3 that I intend to use to develop this Quality	TARGET DATES FOR COMPLETION	ACTUAL COMPLETION DATES
1.			
2.			
3.			
etc.			

Method 2: Conversation with a partner

Although this book is expressly designed for you to work through alone, many of us learn best in dialogue or conversation with others. If this suits you, then first find another person able and prepared to discuss these questions with you.

The advantages of involving someone else as a 'speaking partner' are many. Such people can offer support, and may also be able to give you useful feedback, including challenging some of your assumptions.

You can use the same questions as in Method 1 and as listed in Table 5.1 above. You can also use the same scoring system, and then record your development goals in Table 5.2 – all in dialogue and consultation with your colleague or partner.

Method 3: *The 11 Qualities of the Effective Manager Questionnaire*

The third method for prioritizing your development goals uses *The 11 Qualities of the Effective Manager Questionnaire*, as in Table 5.3 below.

This questionnaire contains 55 items, distributed randomly across the *11 Qualities* as shown in the scoring scheme in Table 5.4, which follows at the end of the chapter.

Scoring

For each of the 55 Item Statements in Table 5.3, score:

0   if the statement is NOT AT ALL TRUE for you

1   if the statement is SLIGHTLY TRUE for you

2   if the statement is QUITE TRUE for you

3   if the statement is VERY TRUE for you

Table 5.3 The 11 Qualities of the Effective Manager Questionnaire

ITEM NUMBER	ITEM STATEMENT	SCORE
1	Experience is the only valid teacher	
2	I have difficulty thinking on my feet in tricky situations	
3	I find that other people don't listen to me properly	
4	I am a shy person – I find it difficult to initiate a conversation with someone I have not met before	
5	I'm not an imaginative person	
6	There are times when other people just don't seem to understand my point of view	
7	I am not able to convert my own experiences into generalized ideas, concepts or theories	
8	I find that I don't know enough about the 'professional and technical' aspects of my job	
9	I find it difficult to think of new ideas	
10	I find that I cannot understand why someone is feeling they way they seem to do	
11	I'm passive rather than active	

(continued)

Table 5.3 (continued)

ITEM NUMBER	ITEM STATEMENT	SCORE
12	I prefer to work on one thing at a time rather than deal with several things at once	
13	I find that I don't seem to know enough about external factors such as market changes, new legislation and the like	
14	I prefer to follow someone else's plans or instructions rather than act on my own initiative	
15	I have difficulty in keeping up with new techniques and developments	
16	I worry about things over and over in my mind	
17	Anger and conflict tend to frighten or upset me	
18	Being introspective is dangerous	
19	I would like to have more theoretical knowledge that would help me in my job	
20	It's difficult to think very far ahead as the immediate goal is more important	
21	I like to temper initiative with caution	
22	I can't see much connection between theory and practice when it comes to management and leadership	
23	I don't seem able to pick up quickly on what's going on	
24	I make plans or decisions only to find later on that they are no longer valid because of something I should have known but didn't	
25	If I hear of a new theory or set of ideas, I find it difficult to translate into practical terms relevant to my job	
26	Compared with how I'd like to be, I think that I am rather slow on the uptake	
27	I have difficulty analysing a situation into its various aspects or parts	
28	When I have a new idea, I like – if possible – to have it checked out by an expert	
29	Generally I don't discuss my feelings or worries with other people	
30	I am better at implementing well-tried solutions rather than experimenting or seeking new ones	
31	I get worried when there's no way of knowing in advance whether or not I have made the right decision	
32	Once I get stuck into a task I try to remain with it rather than switch to something else and then back again	
33	Other people often seem to notice more than I do about what's happening around them	

Table 5.3   (continued)

ITEM NUMBER	ITEM STATEMENT	SCORE
34	Compared with other people, my ideas seem stuck in a rut or fixed by well-established ways of doing things	
35	I find that when something happens, I'm only aware of part of what's going on – I overlook other aspects of the situation or problem	
36	I find it difficult to weigh up the pros and cons of alternative solutions to a problem	
37	I don't spend time thinking about myself – my strengths and areas for improvement	
38	I don't really feel tuned in to what's happening in a situation	
39	I feel a need to have more 'get up and go'	
40	I am not clear about my medium- and long-term aspirations	
41	When I'm under pressure, in a tight spot or being challenged, I can't seem to think straight or express myself clearly	
42	I tend to jump to instant conclusions – acting quickly without spending much time thinking	
43	There's not much point in thinking about oneself – 'contemplating your navel'	
44	I get caught out because I don't know enough about what's happening in my organization or network	
45	I tend to find that I can't make a decision because I don't have enough information	
46	I would like to know more about policies and future plans	
47	When I'm nervous or tired, I snap at people or get moody and irritable	
48	When people have new or unusual ideas, I tend to resist them	
49	I find myself surprised at the way other people react to what's happening	
50	I don't really know who are the important people in my organization or network	
51	Many of the people I work with seem to know more about various aspects or requirements of the job than I do	
52	I don't know enough about what's going on around here	
53	I find myself aware that I'm behaving inappropriately but don't seem able to stop or change the way I'm acting	
54	I don't really know what others think of me	
55	I find it difficult to trust my own judgement	

Scoring the questionnaire

When you have worked through the questionnaire, transfer your scores from the Score column of Table 5.3 to the respective Item Numbers in Table 5.4 below.

Now total up the scores for each of the *11 Qualities* in the right-hand column.

Now look over your total scores. The higher the score, the weaker you see yourself on that particular Quality. As before, you can choose to strengthen your weaker areas, or build on your strengths.

Table 5.4 Scoring key for *The 11 Qualities of the Effective Manager Questionnaire*

The 11 Qualities of the Effective Manager	ITEM NUMBERS					TOTALS
1. Situational facts	24	44	46	50	52	
Score						
2. Professional knowledge and skills	8	13	15	19	51	
Score						
3. Sensitivity to events	23	33	35	38	49	
Score						
4. Analytical skills	27	36	42	45	55	
Score						
5. People skills	3	4	6	10	17	
Score						
6. Emotional resilience	16	29	31	47	53	
Score						
7. Initiative	11	14	20	21	39	
Score						
8. Creativity	5	9	30	34	48	
Score						
9. Mental agility	2	12	26	32	41	
Score						
10. Ability to learn	1	7	22	25	28	
Score						
11. Self-knowledge	18	37	40	43	54	
Score						

If one or two scores are clearly higher than the others, then these might well be your starting priorities for development. If your scores are all similar, however, then choose one or two Qualities to start on by selecting those that appeal to you most.

When you have chosen your one or two priority areas, enter your development goals in Table 5.2. Or, you can write these down as statements of goals perhaps in a *personal journal* (Activity 8 – see Part 3). A good goal statement is specific with regard to action – what will be done, and time – by when, and perhaps by standards – how well willl this be done? For example:

> By (a realistic date) I will have carried out 4 Activities (list numbers) to improve my (e.g. Analytical Skills) and recorded at least 5 key learning outcomes in my Personal journal.

Conclusion

This chapter has offered three ways to help you diagnose your own self-development priorities from which to set realistic learning goals.

In Part 3 of this book, you will find the Activities to help you in achieving these goals. The next chapter, Chapter 6, is a guide to selecting from these Activities for developing each of *The 11 Qualities of the Effective Manager*.

How to Select and Use the Activities

Having chosen your priorities and set yourself some goals, this chapter helps you to select and use appropriate self-development activities from Part 3 of the book.

Selecting the Activities

Table 6.1, *The Qualities and Activities Matrix*, shows *The 11 Qualities of the Effective Manager* in the first column and then lists all 57 Activities for management self-development in columns 2 and 3. Column 2 lists those Activities we think have a *major* application to the quality in question and therefore most likely to help your learning in that particular quality. Column 3 indicates a more *minor* application; so that although the Activity is not primarily designed for that quality, there is likely to be some learning pay-off in this area.

Look for your priority qualities in the first column and choose those activities relevant to your self-development goals. What is the right order in which to tackle activities? This is down to you, but here are three possibilities:

1. One strategy is to start with the activities that help you to 'learn how to learn'. The 'meta-qualities' of self-knowledge, ability to learn, mental agility and creativity – are key to leaders and managers because they promote good self-development habits. These will also help you get the most out of the activities designed for other of *The 11 Qualities of the Effective Manager*.

2. An obvious alternative is to start with your most urgent learning goals, and choose activities appropriate to your greatest area of need.

3. If neither of these appeals to you, you could just dive in and try one or two of the activities, and then make up your mind what to do next as you go along. This 'suck it and see' approach allows you to get a feel for the kind of activities that suit you best.

Table 6.1   The Qualities and Activities Matrix

The 11 Qualities of the Effective Manager	Activities with MAJOR application	Activities with MINOR application
1. Situational facts	1. Know Your Facts 2. Networking	10. Differences and Discrimination 15. Role Set Analysis
2. Professional knowledge and skills	3. Managing Your Time 4. Keeping Up to Date 5. Find a Mentor 6. Communications Tools	10. Differences and Discrimination 14. Planning and Decision Making 18. Critical Thinking 19. Reflective Practice 27. Be a Coach! 28. Virtual Leadership 54. Study Skills
3. Sensitivity to events	7. Facts and Assumptions 8. Personal Journal 9. Use Your Power 10. Differences and Discrimination 11. Political Awareness 12. Credulous Listening	1. Know Your Facts 21. Handing Conflicts 22. Getting the Best Out of Groups 25. Getting to Yes 37. The Virtual Revolution 40. Practising Change 42. Imaging
4. Analytical skills	13. Decision Making 14. Planning and Decision Making 15. Role Set Analysis 16. Planning Change 17. Catastrophic Contingencies 18. Critical Thinking 19. Reflective Practice	3. Managing Your Time 8. Personal Journal 14. Planning and Decision Making 18. Critical Thinking 19. Reflective Practice 22. Getting the Best Out of Groups 23. What Are You Like? 37. The Virtual Revolution 39. Who's the Boss? 41. Action Planning 44. Beyond 'Yes ... But ...' 45. Generating New Ideas
5. People skills	20. Asserting Yourself 21. Handing Conflicts 22. Getting the Best Out of Groups 23. What Are You Like? 24. Getting to Know You 25. Getting to Yes 26. Collaborative Working 27. Be a Coach! 28. Virtual Leadership	2. Networking 6. Communication Tools 7. Facts and Assumptions 9. Use Your Power 11. Political Awareness 12. Credulous Listening 20. Asserting Yourself 28. Virtual Leadership 35. Manage Your Feelings 37. The Virtual Revolution 39. Who's the Boss? 43. Managing Upwards 50. Just a Minute

(continued)

Table 6.1 (*continued*)

The 11 Qualities of the Effective Manager	Activities with MAJOR application	Activities with MINOR application
6. Emotional resilience	29. The Saturated Life 30. Difficult Situations 31. Are You Stressed? 32. Treat Yourself Well 33. Relaxation 34. Fitness 35. Managing Your Feelings 36. Stability Zones 37. The Virtual Revolution 38. Be Your Own Personal Trainer	17. Catastrophic Contingencies 18. Critical Thinking 19. Reflective Practice 20. Asserting Yourself 21. Handing Conflicts 25. Getting to Yes 26. Collaborative Working 40. Practising Change 49. Coping with Complexity
7. Initiative	39. Who's the Boss? 40. Practising Change 41. Action Planning 42. Imaging 43. Managing Upwards	2. Networking 5. Find a Mentor 6. Communications Tools 9. Use Your Power 11. Political Awareness 16. Planning Change 17. Catastrophic Contingencies 20. Asserting Yourself 22. Getting the Best Out of Groups
8. Creativity	44. Beyond 'Yes ... But ...' 45. Generating New Ideas 46. Approaches to Creativity 47. Attribute Alternatives	17. Catastrophic Contingencies 26. Collaborative Working 42. Imaging 48. Your Multiple Intelligences 51. A Helicopter Mind 56. Conversations with Yourself
9. Mental agility	48. Your Multiple Intelligences 49. Coping with Complexity 50. Just a Minute 51. A Helicopter Mind	18. Critical Thinking 19. Reflective Practice
10. Ability to learn	52. Managing Your Dependency 53. Learning to Learn 54. Study Skills 55. Your Learning Cycle	4. Keeping Up to Date 5. Find a Mentor 8. Personal Journal 12. Credulous Listening 27. Be a Coach! 28. Virtual Leadership 51. A Helicopter Mind

Table 6.1 (continued)

The 11 Qualities of the Effective Manager	Activities with MAJOR application	Activities with MINOR application
11. Self-knowledge	56. Conversations with Yourself 57. Backwards Review	7. Facts and Assumptions 8. Personal Journal 17. Catastrophic Contingencies 20. Asserting Yourself 23. What Are You Like? 24. Getting to Know You 29. The Saturated Life 31. Are You Stressed? 32. Treat Yourself Well 35. Manage Your Feelings 38. Be Your Own Personal Trainer 44. Beyond 'Yes ... But ...' 47. Attribute Alternatives 53. Learning to Learn 54. Study Skills 55. Your Learning Cycle

Using the Activities

There are many paths to self-development. Opportunities commonly found in large organizations include:

- mentoring
- coaching/counselling
- appraisal
- internal rotation, attachments and placements
- external attachments and placements
- reading
- joining special projects
- committee membership
- discussion groups, working parties, meetings of professional bodies and institutes
- learning from one's own job and experience
- special activities.

In smaller organizations, or if you are self-employed, you will need to generate your own learning opportunities. Here local networks and professional organizations such as the ILM – the

Institute of Leadership & Management – can be vital in helping you reach like-minded people with an interest in development and education.

However, even in relatively well-resourced organizations, your work experiences may not lead to development or learning. Some of these possibilities, such as committee work or professional gatherings, may be too predictable and routine, whereas others, such as appraisal sessions, may be used more to control and direct people rather than be focused on development. However, you can often influence this more than you may think. Most work experiences can be rendered rewarding with effort and ingenuity, and we recommend that you scan all of the self-development opportunities open to you and take advantage of those that you think will work best for you. This book will help you to learn from all these possibilities.

Whatever your circumstances and possibilities, this book provides you with a 'starter pack' of Activities to use in your self-development programme. The following notes will help you to get the most out of them.

Commitment

It is said that the more you put in, the more you get out. Physical fitness activities can't work if you only pretend to do them, or do them half-heartedly, and it's the same with the self-development activities in this book. There is little point in cheating yourself. Here are two ways to support your commitment:

■ *Working with a partner*. All the Activities in this book can be done on your own, but you might get more benefit by working with a partner – a colleague or a friend. It matters less who the partner is than they are someone you can trust, who will listen to you and give you honest feedback. If you decide to work with a partner, then 'Getting to Know You' (Activity 24) might be a good start on building a helping relationship.

■ *Working with a group*. A few people trying the Activities together can be very motivating and good fun. Again if you are in a large organization, your training and development managers might be able to help you form such a group. Alternatively, you could set up your own development group by inviting some colleagues or friends to join you. 'Collaborative Working' (Activity 26) will help you do this.

Action and Learning

Each Activity in *A Manager's Guide to Self-development* is built around a three-stage model of learning (Figure 6.1):

■ *What?* is the experience following the action. Each Activity proposes some action, and also asks you to note your experiences of what happens. Writing down your observations and reactions is the first step in learning from experience.

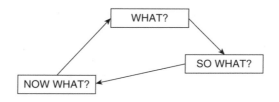

Figure 6.1 Doing the Activities

- *So what?* means thinking about what has happened, and analysing your reactions and observations. What are your feelings? Ideas? Insights? Questions? This involves you reflecting on your experiences and making sense of them.

- *Now what?* is the most difficult bit. This means taking stock of your actions and your learning and deciding how this will change your behaviour. *Now what?* implies concrete plans for personal change based on your learning. It is very important to write these down, for they are the basis for your ongoing self-development.

Make the Activities part of your normal life

Doing all the Activities in Part 3 of *A Manager's Guide to Self-development* may not immediately make you the perfect manager or leader. But we can guarantee that doing them will kick-start your self-development and encourage you in a learning process that will have a major impact on your life.

Make these Activities part of your normal working life. Incorporate these good learning habits into your everyday work. You might do this by repeating certain Activities that are particularly significant for you; for with repetition you will notice how your skills and abilities are growing and progressing. You can use the 'Personal Journal' (Activity 8) to keep track of this progress.

In working with these Activities, perhaps modifying them and generating your own approaches, and by seeing your everyday experiences as opportunities for self-development, you will become what someone once called a 'learning manager', and this book will have achieved its purpose.

PART 3

Activities for Management Self-development

Know Your Facts

Managerial qualities	Situational facts: Sensitivity to events

All work involves making decisions and putting them into practice. Facts are inputs to decisions. However good you are at decision making, your decisions and actions will be wrong if they are based on inaccurate information. Situational facts include such things as the price of materials, the size of an order book or a customer's delivery deadline. Professional knowledge is to do with specialist management such as information management or financial reporting requirements.

Situational facts can be distinguished from professional knowledge and skills, because this is the input to *managerial* rather than *professional* decisions. The manager of a plant with a sophisticated technology may have a technical background sufficient to make *managerial* decisions, to plan, for instance, the plant's output and staffing, taking account of the need for maintenance. If the plant breaks down technically, the manager may choose to get involved in the technical/professional search for a solution, but this is a temporary return to a technical/professional role. Here we are concerned with situational facts as an input to managerial decisions.

Situational facts vary in terms of their permanence, from highly variable, such as the price of services and the stock level of finished goods, to relatively permanent, say, the date of annual audit or the preferences of regular customers.

Reviewing your command of situational facts

Once you have identified what you need to know in developing your command of situational facts, it is probably fairly easy to get this knowledge. The problem is that we usually don't know what we don't know, and it is the data in the blind spots that we really need.

Consider the situation shown in Figure A1.1.

What you need to do is to convert Cs into As, Ds into Bs, and Bs into As.

The exercise below will help you to clarify what you already have in 'A' and 'B', add to it from 'C', and help you explore 'D'.

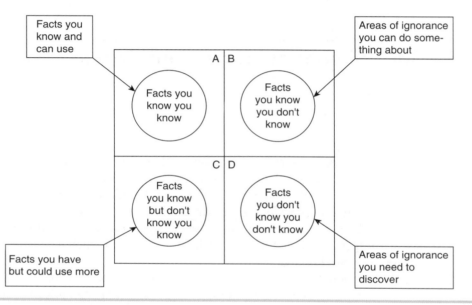

Figure A1.1 Four types of facts

Activity

Step 1

Imagine that someone important wants to check whether you are really on the ball on the situational facts concerning your job or role.

Take a piece of paper and write down as many key questions as you can think of about any facts of your job as it exists now. Imagine that you are compiling

the test questions for *Mastermind*, with your job as the topic. Aim to get at least 10 or 12. Now write down all the answers to these questions.

Step 2

Now extend the list of questions and answers by any or all of the following:

(a) If you redesigned, developed or extended your job in any way that you think desirable, what would this add to the list of questions and answers?
(b) What are the next possible moves in your career? What new facts would you need to have at your command to perform these future jobs?
(c) What kind of training and education are provided for people coming into your kind of work? What facts do they have that you don't have?
(d) Imagine showing your list to:
   (i) your boss
  (ii) your staff
 (iii) your colleagues
 (iv) others in similar jobs to yourself
  (v) anyone else with whom you are regularly in contact.

What do you think they might suggest that you add to the list?
(e) Show your list to some of the people mentioned in (d) and ask them. Exchange lists with someone in a similar job to yourself who has done this exercise and discuss them both.

N.B. Point (e) is particularly important because of the 'don't-know-what-you-don't-know' factor; so second opinions greatly enhance the benefit you can get from this activity.

Follow-up

You probably know the answers to most of the new questions you have posed, but make a list of things you need to know about the others.

If any of them strike you as difficult, then other activities in this book related to the Managerial Qualities 'Sensitivity to events' and 'Ability to learn' (Table 6.1) will help.

Networking

Managerial qualities	**Situational facts:** People skills: Initiative

The effective manager knows not only 'what's what', but also 'who's who'. 'The old boys' network' has often attracted anger partly because it has proved so effective for 'old boys' wanting to get on. Even more so today, networking has become an essential task and skill for all managers because so much depends upon good relationships and upon knowing where to connect with the distributed knowledge on any issue. To be effective we need a lot of contacts; we need to know what others do, how they can help us and how we can help them.

Activity

Step 1

The first step is to decide whom you are going to get to know. To start with, choose one person to get to know better and find out what they do. There are a number of ways of doing this. For example:

1. Look at an organization chart and choose someone in an area about which you know very little.
2. Use an internal telephone directory to the same end.
3. Pick a person from the offices or workplaces around you.

4. Choose someone whom you have seen about the place, without knowing who they are or what they do.

5. Choose a person at random, the third person who enters a lift or walks into the canteen, or stick a pin into the internal telephone book.

Step 2

Having chosen your first potential contact, start to get to know him or her.

This will be more difficult than it sounds, but less difficult than you imagine. You can explain frankly that you are trying to get to know more people or, if you prefer a more covert approach, just try to engage the chosen person in informal conversation.

Your goal should be to find answers to the following questions:

(a) What is the person's name?
(b) What is his or her job title?
(c) What does that job involve?
(d) How does this person see the main purpose of the job and its contribution to the organization? (Do you agree? If not, can you explore this difference?)
(e) What are his or her major goals, concerns, issues, problems?
(f) In what way can the person be of help to you?
(g) In what way can you be of help to him or her?
(h) Are there any ways in which the person's goals, needs or interests conflict with yours? If so, what can be done to lessen or overcome this conflict?

You will need to develop certain skills to get the person talking about these things. Some hints on how to do this are given in Table A2.1.

Step 3

Once you have made your first contact, repeat the activity, perhaps meeting at least one new person a week until you feel you have built your network to a good level.

Follow-up

Quintessential Careers (http://www.quintcareers.com/networking.html) is a useful website that offers links to many career networking websites. There you will be directed to various categories of site, including for example those aimed at professionals, women and those concerned with diversity issues. You will

Table A2.1   **Hints on getting another person to talk freely**

1. If you want fairly long, descriptive answers, ask open-ended questions, such as:

   'What ... ?'

   'How do you ... ?'

   'Could you explain ... ?'

   'Can you give an example of ... ?'

   'How do you feel about ... ?'

   'Why do you ... ?'

2. Unless you want very specific, precise, short answers, avoid closed questions, such as:

   'Do you ... ?'

   'How often ... ?'

   'Is it true that ... ?'

   'How many ... ?'

3. Notice non-verbal cues, such as tone of voice, changes in posture, facial expression, eye movement, gestures, speech hesitancies.

4. Respond to non-verbal cues by using them to suggest further questions, by remarking on them, or by changing the subject, whichever you think most appropriate.

5. Check out and clarify what you are hearing (i.e. repeat in your own words what you think the other person has said, what is meant and how he or she feels).

6. If the other person talks mostly about feelings, it might be useful to ask about ideas or facts; on the other hand, if facts are offered at the time, then try asking about feelings.

7. From time to time, find out the other person's feelings about you and the process of the discussion.

8. All the time, ask yourself if you are prepared to be as open with the other person as you are asking him or her to be with you.

also find articles, papers and general networking tools that are available on the web.

www.networking-coach.com is a Dutch networking consultant's site – with a version available in English. There is an e-learning course delivered by email, which, at the time of writing, is free. Well worth a try if you are interested.

Gael and Stuart Lindenfield's *Confident Networking for Career Success and Satisfaction* (Piatkus, 2010) is an easy read on general career networking, while *Leadership Networking: Connect, Collaborate, Create* by Curt Grayson and David Baldwin (Center for Creative Leadership, 2007) has a special emphasis on networking as a critical leadership skill. Both are available electronically on Kindle.

Managing Your Time

Managerial qualities	**Professional knowledge and skills:** Situational facts: Analytical skills

Time is a major scarcity for twenty-first-century people. The opportunities for time spending become more numerous every year. We consume more and more and although we have time-saving devices, they also demand time for maintenance. We have to budget time as we budget money. We calculate the opportunity cost of spending time even with friends, relatives and loved ones.

Make a quick inventory of your free time for the rest of the week:

	Hours
Monday	
Tuesday	
Wednesday	
Thursday	
Friday	
Saturday	
Sunday	

Note down how much free time you have each day. What is left after sleeping, eating, working and travelling? Then try jotting down things you could do in this time, under three headings:

1. Things I MUST do this week.

_____

_____

_____

_____

2. Things I SHOULD do this week.

_____

_____

_____

_____

3. Things I would LIKE to do this week (if only I had the time).

_____

_____

_____

_____

As this is a private list and for your eyes only, you can afford to be honest with yourself.

For example, have you included time for being with close friends and family? Time for doing nothing much? Time to recover from doing too much? Time for passing the time of day with all those other faces and acquaintances in your life?

A main purpose of the activity below is to gain some feeling of control over how your time is spent. This might involve cutting out unrewarding activities but it might also include looking for chunks of time in which to do things which you're not doing at the moment but which you ought or would like to be doing.

For example, a manager in a large retail company looked at the way she used working time. She discovered that she spent _three hours every day_ overseeing

and checking the work of her staff (and another hour each day taking lunch). On top of her own busy job, she had staff members who didn't accept responsibility and who did not exercise initiative. She had a weight problem, because she never had enough time to take exercise. What she could not see was that the way she spent time was linked to her other problems. How could members of staff exercise responsibility if she gave them no discretion – if their work was continuously checked? She could have gained another half hour by having a light lunch and a walk instead of her usual one-hour three-courser in the management dining room.

So, managing your time properly may increase others' effectiveness and capacity in addition to your own. It is also one of the keys to the thorny problem of delegation – are you spending your time on the right activities? We can see you're busy – but doing what?

Activity

Managing time is one aspect of leading yourself. One of the 11 Qualities of the Effective Manager and leader is *initiative* – being a self-starter, taking personal responsibility and getting something done. You can start here – in three steps:

1. *Recording* how your time is spent. (Before you can manage your time, you need to find out what you're doing with it.)
2. *Analysing* what you spend your time on.
3. *Making decisions* about the most effective use of your discretionary time.

Step 1

Record your activities at work for the next five days. You can design your own recording sheet or use the one given in Table A3.1.

Spend five days, *at least*, on this – the full value of the exercise cannot be gained from less.

Step 2

When you have at least five days' worth of data, analyse your data sheets under four headings:

(a) *outcome*
(b) *type of work*
(c) *where does the work come from?*
(d) *delegation.*

Table A3.1   Recording sheet

		TIME LOG		
Day:_____ Date:_____				
Describe WHAT HAPPENS in detail – the subject of meetings, phone calls, letters, reading, conversations. Note the DURATION of each happening. Note the NAME and POSITION of OTHER PEOPLE INVOLVED. Include even casual encounters.				
Time	What happened?	Duration	People involved	Comments
9.00 9.30				
9.30 10.00				
10.00 10.30				
10.30 11.00				
11.00 11.30				
11.30 12.00				
12.00 12.30				
12.30 1.00				
1.00 1.30				
1.30 2.00				
2.00 2.30				
2.30 3.00				
3.00 3.30				
3.30 4.00				
4.00 4.30				
4.30 5.00				
5.00				

(a) OUTCOME

■ How successful were the various activities?

_____

_____

_____

_____

■ Have you any habitual failures?

_____

_____

_____

(b) TYPE OF WORK

Divide your work tasks into three categories:

■ MUST do? (most important duties)

_____

_____

_____

■ SHOULD do? (next most important duties)

_____

_____

_____

■ Would LIKE to do? (least important duties)

_____

_____

_____

Allocate a theoretical percentage of your effort to each of these, for example, 75%, 20% or 5%.

How much of your time are you spending on each set of activities compared with the 'correct' theoretical mix?

N.B. We often concentrate on things we are able to do or like doing at the expense of things that we find difficult. These difficult tasks may be the most vital ones.

Another way of looking at this is to ask yourself what proportion of my time goes on:

■ *Leadership and managerial work* – planning, motivating, team building, etc.?

_____

_____

_____

■ *Professional skills* – exercising your own specialist professional skills?

_____

_____

_____

A common trap is the carrying over of professional work into the manager's job. You may need to exercise these skills part of the time, but exactly how much is appropriate:

10%?
15%?
20%?

And how much are you *actually* doing?

The *leadership and managerial* work may be the most difficult and you may be avoiding it – preferring the comfort of working in your old craft or field.

(c) WHERE DOES THE WORK COME FROM? From the . . .

■ Boss – is he or she delegating enough? or too much is he or she using you as a personal assistant?

_____

_____

_____

■ Staff – are they too dependent upon you?

_____

_____

_____

■ Self – are you setting yourself enough tasks?

_____

_____

_____

■ Elsewhere – where?

_____

_____

_____

How important are each of these?

(d) DELEGATION

For each task or event ask yourself:

■ Could this have been delegated?
■ If YES, to whom?

If NO, why not? (Your answer to this one should be really thoughtful.) Is it really your job or have you made yourself indispensable?

Step 3

After analysis it's time to make some decisions about how to spend your time.

(a) What things are you spending time on that you could either **cut out, cut down, or delegate**?
(b) What things are you not doing now that you should be – or what things should you **be doing more of**?

You can use your three job areas of MUST DO, SHOULD DO and WOULD LIKE to do for this.
  Make sure the MUST DOs are done!

(c) What actions will you **commit yourself to here and now**?

Action

1. *Completed by:*

_____

_____

_____

2. *Completed by:*

_____

_____

_____

3. *Completed by:*

_____

_____

_____

4. *Completed by:*

_____

_____

_____

etc.

Obviously, you can repeat your time log any time you like to check how you're functioning, when are your best times, and so on.

Follow-up

There are numerous self-help books on time management, and typing 'time management' into a search engine will produce literally millions of hits. You

can also get software products for time management that support multiple users allowing for the allocation of tasks and the use of the software for communication and coordination.

However, be warned. Time management materials tend to make very rational and linear assumptions, and accordingly offer simple and standard solutions. If these worked for everyone, there would not be such a big market out there. Take task lists, for example, which one of us uses, but the other two don't. It has been suggested that 30% of 'listers' spend more time managing their lists than they do completing the tasks themselves!

Dartmouth University has a well-known suite of time management materials aimed at helping students to maximize their study potential: http://www.dartmouth.edu/ ~ acskills/success/time.html.

MindTools.com has a whole range of devices listed under the headings of Prioritization, Scheduling, Time Management Challenges, Self-motivation, Concentration & Focus & Goal Setting: www.mindtools.com/pages/main/newMN_HTE.htm.

Time Management for Dummies by Clare Evans (Wiley, 2008 and Kindle edition, 2011) is near universally praised as a simple and straightforward guide. *The Time Trap: The Classic Book on Time Management* by Pat Nickerson and Alec Mackenzie (Amacom, 2009) is a fourth edition of a classic.

Keeping Up to Date

Managerial qualities	**Professional knowledge and skills:** Ability to learn

Successful leaders and managers know what is going on. Good judgement rests on up-to-date professional knowledge. A good manager or leader needs to know not only about new developments in their specialist expertise but more generally about changes in markets, legislation, culture, fashions, and so on. The purpose of this activity is to encourage you to think about your personal strategy for keeping up to date and to suggest some ways of doing this.

Activity

Step 1

First, here are some questions to answer. Take your time and think about them before you answer.

(a) How much time do you spend READING in your field each week?

_____

_____

_____

(b) How much time do you spend LOOKING AT WEBSITES, USING ELECTRONIC CONFERENCES, NOTICE BOARDS, etc.?

_____

_____

_____

(c) How would you describe the way you read this material (e.g. scanning, gleaning, immersing yourself)?

_____

_____

_____

(d) Write down the names of the JOURNALS, NEWSLETTERS, WEBSITES, ELECTRONIC CONFERENCES, etc., that you use regularly.

_____

_____

_____

(e) Which relevant JOURNALS, MAGAZINES, NEWSLETTERS, WEBSITES, etc., do you *not* see or read?

_____

_____

_____

(f) Do you ever make use of TRAINING PACKAGES, that is, manuals, interactive videos, online learning or web-based learning resources?

_____

_____

_____

(g) Do you ever make use of ON-LINE LEARNING?

_____

_____

_____

(h) Write down the PROFESSIONAL BODIES or ASSOCIATIONS to which you belong, and any Continuing Professional Development (CPD) support provided by them that you use.

_____

_____

_____

(i) Write down which COURSES and CONFERENCES you have attended in the last year.

_____

_____

_____

(j) Have you made any VISITS or STUDY TOURS in the last year?

_____

_____

_____

(k) What other ways of developing your professional knowledge and skills have you used in the last year?

_____

_____

_____

Step 2

Now look over your answers to these questions. What sort of a picture do you get? Is CPD at the bottom of your pile of priorities or are you taking it seriously? Do you have a strategy for the future?

Keeping up to date can easily get neglected because it is not a crisis issue. Its effects are cumulative and insidious over time, the error realized only several years later. Putting time into your CPD is investing in your business – you don't get a good crop of beans without a generous investment of manure.

Now examine your answers in more detail. Many of them concern the activity of reading and using material from e-resources. Even now in the digital age this is an essential part of keeping up to date for most of us. One way to make sure that we do enough professional reading and gain most benefit from it is to read *purposefully*.

Step 3

Choose something to read – a paper, article, book chapter or web-based text. Find a time and place when you can sit down and read it.

Now review your reading using the questions in Table A4.1. Some sample answers are given, but make sure you provide your own.

Reviewing your reading will give you an insight into how you go about it. For example:

■ *Why* do you read (and why *don't* you)? (To glean or ransack; to escape; to meditate on, etc.)

_____

_____

_____

■ *When* do you read? (What's the best time and place for you?)

_____

_____

_____

■ *What* do you do when you get bored, lose the thread or disagree with what's written? (Give up; take a break; get angry; eat a sandwich, etc.)

_____

_____

_____

■ For *how long* can you/do you read?

_____

_____

_____

Table A4.1   **Reading review**

Reading review questions	Some sample answers
1. For how long did I read?	– For 5 minutes, then I was interrupted
	– For half an hour
	– For 10 minutes, until I became exasperated with the author's views
2. Did I skim or jump forwards?	– No, I plodded through
	– Yes, I skimmed it first
	– Yes, because I couldn't understand that bit or because I knew that bit
3. Did I go back and re-read bits?	– Yes, I re-read when I couldn't understand
	– No, I just kept reading on
	– Yes, because a later bit reminded me of an earlier bit and so I checked back
4. Did I pause at all?	– Yes, I needed to think about an idea I had while reading
	– Yes, I needed a break
	– No, I made myself continue
5. Did I take notes?	– Yes, just main headings and definitions
	– No, I don't need to remember any of this
	– Yes, it's just habit with me
6. What was my purpose in reading?	– To extract practical ideas
	– To check my level of understanding in this field
	– To memorize for an examination
	– To decide whether to buy or borrow it

We all have our own reading patterns and preferences. Understanding your reading habits means that you will know when to read what sort of material for what purpose.

Step 4

Now choose another paper, book chapter or web-based text. Find time and space to read it. Before you start, note down the following:

■ Your purpose in reading this.

_____

_____

_____

■ How much time you have for reading.

_____

_____

_____

■ Whether or not you will take notes.

_____

_____

_____

■ Whether or not you will skim it first.

_____

_____

_____

■ Where you will do your reading.

_____

_____

_____

■ What you will do when you get bored/frustrated, etc.

_____

_____

_____

Now read. Take the time to review again using the questions in Step 3. Are your patterns becoming clearer?

Step 5

The questions in Step 1 (d) and (e) are about paper or electronic JOURNALS, MAGAZINES and NEWSLETTERS, which are an important source of up-to-date knowledge. Journal and magazine articles often lead books in opening up new knowledge by several years.

Take the lists you made in Step 1 (d) and (e) to your librarian or resource centre or to a knowledgeable friend. (If you haven't got access to any of these, that should tell you something about your keeping up-to-date strategy – perhaps a first step would be to find one?)

Ask your librarian or friend to check your lists and to add to your question (d) list if possible. Is there any comment on your choices? Can you be put on a 'circulation list' for any recommended journals? There are often plenty of journals, newsletters, etc., around which don't get read by many people because they are not well circulated.

In this way, you can begin to build up a circulating network, 'papernet' or e-mailing group where you swap items of mutual interest with professional colleagues.

Step 6

Step 1, questions (f) and (g) ask about your use of PACKAGES and ON-LINE LEARNING. These are increasingly available for busy managers and if you are fortunate enough to work in an organization with a training department, then this is the place to start. In addition to making demands on your training person, you can also try the local college or university where there may be learning resources centres.

Step 7

Question (h) in Step 1 asks about membership of PROFESSIONAL BODIES and ASSOCIATIONS. Professional bodies not only organize conferences and branch meetings where you can meet other members, but also circulate newsletters and journals. Many professional bodies encourage or even demand 'continuous professional development' and provide resources for this. You can contact them for lists of relevant packages and resources. For example, the BIM (British Institute of Management) has an excellent education information unit that will answer queries about all sorts of professional development activities.

Step 8

COURSES, CONFERENCES and VISITS are another way of updating and learning. Courses are the most common way of keeping up to date. However, they are not designed specifically for you, and people often get sent on them rather than choosing them for themselves. Make sure you choose yourself, and know why you're going.

Step 9

Have you any other ideas for keeping up to date? As we often stress in this book, COLLEAGUES are one of the best sources of up-to-date information. To generate some fresh thoughts, go round your colleagues – how do they keep themselves up to date? And, what's new?

Step 10

A *strategy for keeping up to date*. After considering all these methods, how are you going to ensure you stay up to date? It is best to have a strategy consisting of two parts:

(a) *Choose* which methods of keeping up to date you will follow in, say, the next six months.
(b) *Plan* when, where and how you will do these chosen activities. Use a table like that in Activity 41, *Action Planning*, to help you do this. It is also a good idea to find a colleague or confidant with whom you can share your plan and review progress from time to time. This helps a lot.

Follow-up

Key Management Models: The 60+ Models Every Manager Needs to Know by Marcel Van Assen, Gerben Van den Berg and Paul Pietersma (FT/Prentice-Hall, 2nd edition, 2009) is a quick guide to well-known business models with three or four pages of explanation on each.

Your own professional body is a good place to start keeping up to date. Professional institutions often publish up-to-date summaries on recent trends,

happenings and changes. The ILM (Institute of Leadership and Management) is aimed at all managers and leaders and has information about development activities and publishes an annual analysis of leadership trust at www.i-l-m.com.

Internet search engines are also useful, but you can be overwhelmed by irrelevance. *Search Engine Watch* at http://searchenginewatch.com is updated daily. It is aimed at people who really *are* interested in search engines and you can become a member and sign up for a newsletter, but it also contains information to help you use the web more efficiently.

Find a Mentor

Managerial qualities	**Professional knowledge and skills:** Ability to learn: Initiative

Being mentored – for a new job, a different role or a demanding task – is one of the best ways to learn. If you don't have a mentor, why not get yourself one?

Mentoring overlaps with coaching and this confusion is not helped by the fact that different definitions are used for both. Generally, whereas coaches tend to focus on specific problems or skills in the shorter term, mentors take a broader focus on the wider development of the person within a life or career. Table A5.1 outlines these differences in more detail, contrasting the mentor role with that of the coach and the more traditional instructor.

It may be that these terms are used differently in your organization, perhaps reversing the definitions of coaching and mentoring, or using additional descriptions such as 'business mentoring' or 'life coaching'. Modify the table to suit your needs and to reflect the language used in your organization. It will then help you to understand the options and to ensure that understanding is shared with any prospective mentor.

Activity

This activity will help you to think through what you want from a mentor and get you started on a mentoring relationship.

Table A5.1   Instructor, coach or mentor?

Three ways of being helped to learn: Instructor, coach or mentor			
Dimension	**Instructor**	**Coach**	**Mentor**
Focus of help	Task	Job results	Development of person over career or life
Timespan	A day or two	A month to a year	Career or lifetime
Approach to helping	'Show and tell' – give supervised practice	Explore problem together and set up opportunities to try out new skills	Act as friend willing to play 'devil's advocate' – listen and question to increase awareness
Associated activities	Analysing task: clear instruction, practice, give feedback on results at once	Jointly identify the problem: create development opportunity and review	Link work with other parts of life: clarify long-term aims and purpose in life
Ownership	Helper	Shared	Learner
Attitude to ambiguity	Eliminate	Use it as a challenge – as a puzzle to solve	Accept as part of life and of the world
Benefits to the business	Standard, competent performance	Goal-directed performance oriented to improvement and being creative	Conscious questioning approach to the business purpose

Note: Adapted from the original by David Megginson.

Step 1: Who has helped me to learn?

First write down the names of the people in your life who have helped you to learn important things – go back as far as you can:

1.
2.
3.
4.
5.
etc.

Now reflect on the following questions:

■   What do these people have in common?

_____

_____

_____

■ What did I receive from these people?

_____

_____

_____

■ What do I look for in such people?

_____

_____

_____

Step 2: What do I need now?

Step 1 should have given you some clues about what you look for in a mentor. Perhaps this has been different for you at different times in your life? Many of us look for clear advice and guidance at the start of our career, whereas later on we may look more for support and challenge of our ideas and proposals. Here are three more questions to ponder about what you want:

■ What career/life stage are you at now?

_____

_____

_____

■ What sort of help for learning do you need now?

_____

_____

_____

■ Assuming that you have found the right person, describe what you would like to receive from the relationship.

_____

_____

_____

Step 3: Finding a mentor

A mentor may be someone from within your organization but can be from outside. It is usually best not to choose someone who has any line management relationship with you. Beware of any conflicts of interest in looking for a mentor and if you choose one in your own organization, it is often better to look for one outside of your immediate area.

Now list all the possible people that you might choose. Don't be inhibited by thoughts about whether they will agree or not, just write down who you think you would like:

1.
2.
3.
4.
5.
etc.

If you get stuck on this list, ask a friend, or talk it over with your manager – can they suggest other good people?

Now put your list in order of priority – who is at the top?

Step 4: Making contact

Contact your preferred person. Ask them if they can spare you half an hour to talk about your career.

Having the courage to make contact will be a hard step for many people, but remember that you are only asking for a half hour of their time at this stage.

In your discussion with this person (and others on your list), make sure that you cover the following:

- What sort of help are you looking for?
- When, where, for how often and for how long will you meet?
- What might be in this relationship for the other person?
- Fix the date of the next meeting.

In discussing these questions with your prospective mentor, it might be helpful to use Table A5.1 again to help check that they share the same perception of what is being described.

Good luck.

Follow-up

This activity complements many others in this book, especially Activity 27, *Be a Coach!*, where the Follow-up references there will also be useful here. *Coaching and Mentoring at Work* by Mary Connor and Julia Pokora (Open University/McGraw-Hill, 2nd edition, 2012) is particularly strong on ethical issues and developing good practice, while David Megginson and David Clutterbuck's *Techniques for Coaching and Mentoring* (Kindle edition, 2012) is another well-proven guide. The prolific Jenny Rogers also has a new book: *Manager as Coach: The New Way to Get Results* (McGraw-Hill, 2012), which provides a practical framework and a step-by-step guide to coaching skills for managers.

A visit to the web will throw up thousands of offerings on mentoring. The European Mentoring and Coaching Council (EMCC), which brings together practitioners, researchers and institutions and is attempting to regulate this new profession, is a good place to start: www.emccouncil.org.

Communication Tools

Managerial qualities	**Professional knowledge and skills:** People skills: Initiative

Do you find it easy to choose the appropriate media for communications at work?

The number and variety of communication possibilities and media increase year on year – as do the possibilities for their inappropriate use. There are infamous examples of intimate e-mails circulating around global corporations or reaching the world's press within hours, but more mundane illustrations can be found in every workplace. People write about tricky issues when they could walk ten yards and discuss them; we call expensive meetings to transact administrative matters or hold decision-making sessions without prior agreement on agendas or circulation of relevant papers.

Do you understand which communications tool to use in what circumstances?

Activity

Step 1

Consider the ten sorts of communications situations below.

Against each, note the medium or communications method that you would use for that situation:

Communications situations:

Appropriate communications method(s):

1. Transmission of simple data
2. Transmission of complex data
3. Making arrangements
4. Updating/keeping in touch
5. Sounding out opinions on tricky issues
6. Sorting out personal differences
7. Sorting out group conflicts
8. Making complex decisions
9. General networking
10. Communicating praise and support

Step 2

Now compare your answers with the suggestions in Table A6.1.

This matrix lists some of the main communications media across the top and the types of communication down the left-hand side.

Ticks and crosses show the recommended and non-recommended media for particular types of communication. Question marks indicate possibilities and queries.

Table A6.1 A communications matrix

	E-mail or letter	Personal phone call	One-to-one meeting	Phone or video conference	Group meeting
1. Transmission of simple data	✓	?	×	×	×
2. Transmission of complex data	✓	×	✓	?	?
3. Making arrangements	✓	✓	×	×	×
4. Updating/keeping in touch	✓	✓	✓	?	?
5. Sounding out opinions on tricky issues	✓	✓	✓	?	?
6. Sorting out personal differences	×	?	✓	×	×
7. Sorting out group conflicts	×	×	×	?	✓
8. Making complex decisions	?	?	✓	✓	✓
9. General networking	×	?	✓	×	×
10. Communicating praise and support	✓	✓	✓	✓	✓

Step 3

How did you do? Do you think you have a good sense of what to use in which circumstances?

Some types of communication situations are fairly straightforward (e.g. 1–4 in the matrix); others are fraught with danger (e.g. 6–8 in the matrix). Take special care with these latter types.

No tool can do full justice to the almost infinite variety of human communications possibilities. For example, this tool does not cover those useful informal communications settings, such as the 'corridor meeting' or chatting in social spaces such as dining rooms or bars. These can be the most effective places to transact sensitive or 'unstructured' business.

Follow-up

The Communications Matrix tool is there to be consulted, not slavishly followed. It can be used in team meetings to agree the appropriate communications medium for any action. Pin it above your desk and consult it whenever you are in any doubt.

Most books on communication – and there are many – aim to make it as simple and straightforward as possible. Gill Hasson's *Brilliant Communication Skill: What the Best Communicators Know, Do & Say* (Pearson, 2012) is straightforward and readable.

Facts and Assumptions

Managerial qualities	**Sensitivity to events:** Self-knowledge: People skills

We rarely bother to separate facts from assumptions. Entering my office in the morning, I observe facts and make assumptions. I observe that the office door is shut, but I assume much more: that the room has been cleaned; that the papers I left on my desk last night are still there; that the furniture is arranged as I left it; and so on. Assumptions nearly always outweigh observations. When I go to a meeting, I observe that certain people are present, but I make assumptions: how certain individuals will behave; how long the meeting will last; whether I will be interested or bored; and so on.

This ability to assume and predict is an important human skill, without which progress would be painfully slow and limited. However, when I make wrong assumptions, and act accordingly, I make mistakes. If I think my ideas might be attacked at a meeting, I might decide that attacking first is the best form of defence. When I am attacked, my assumption is confirmed. Or is it? This is the *Self-fulfilling Prophecy* – I made an assumption and acted on it, this action causes the effect, which confirms my original but false assumption.

Another problem is that if we have already made assumptions about how things are, we may not observe certain facts that do not fit with those assumptions. This is 'selective perception'. We see what we want to see; select those things we are looking for and select out others. Enter a room looking for a book and you probably won't notice the new furniture arrangement. This activity will help to build the mental muscles to distinguish facts from assumptions.

Activity

Step 1

Choose a person who is new to your organization, or whom you have only just met.

Step 2

Observe this person and list all those things that you can verify as *facts*: dress, appearance, expressions, behaviour, and so on.

Philosophically, it is perhaps impossible to justify anything as a fact, but there are some things about which we can be relatively certain: 'He is very tall' (of a 6'3" man), for instance. But how factual is the statement 'She is very nice'? (Even 'very tall' is subjective and may not be regarded as fact when talking about basketball players.) The safest rule is to ask yourself: 'What will I accept as a fact, that is a given or commonly verifiable piece of information, in this particular situation?'

Step 3

Now make a second list of *assumptions*. These may be based upon the facts you have observed, but they should be assumptions, guesses or predictions arising out of those facts on such matters as status, religion, likes or dislikes, personality problems, marital status, habits, opinions, attitudes, and so on.

Some of these assumptions may be relatively safe: it is a fact that she is tall, therefore it is fair to assume that 'she finds the office desks uncomfortable to sit at'. Or they might be more 'risky'. 'She is tall', therefore can one assume 'her husband is tall also', or 'she feels embarrassed at being so tall'? Be honest with yourself and list all the assumptions that come to mind.

Step 4

When you have made your list of assumptions, estimate how many will be correct. If possible, check these out with the person, explaining the object of the exercise. Whatever happens, you will have made a new acquaintance and possibly a friend!

What proportion of your assumptions were correct?

If you can't pluck up the courage to approach the person in question, you could ask a friend or colleague to go through the same activity and compare lists.

What did you observe that your friend did not, and vice versa? What assumptions did each of you make?

Step 5

Finally, reflect on what you have learned from this activity. Write a few notes for yourself under each of the four questions below:

(a) What did you learn about the nature of 'facts'?

_____

_____

_____

(b) What did you learn about the number of assumptions you habitually make about people and situations?

_____

_____

_____

(c) Did you discover how selective your perception is?

_____

_____

_____

(d) Can you think of other situations at work where you go through similar facts – assumptions, connections?

_____

_____

_____

You can repeat this activity with any number of suitable people. An interesting variation is to study the next meeting or interview you attend. Draw up lists of 'facts' and 'assumptions' beforehand and observe during the event and check back on your lists afterwards. If you do this once or twice, you might be

surprised at (i) how observant you're becoming, (ii) how accurate your assumptions are becoming, and (iii) how cautious you are now about making assumptions!

Follow-up

The theory that we 'socially construct' our worlds together in our everyday activities is particularly relevant to life in organizations. Wikipedia will give you a start on this topic and also help you to distinguish 'constructionism' from 'constructivism'. The Taos Institute (www.taosinstitute.net) publishes guides on various aspects of social construction, and also runs workshops and other programmes.

Many of the books on this topic are tough to read but Ken Gergen's *An Invitation to Social Construction* (Sage, 2nd edition, 2009) is both accessible and theoretically sound. Vivien Burr's *Social Constructionism* (Routledge, 2nd edition, 2003) is aimed at students and is now available on Kindle.

Personal Journal

Managerial qualities	**Sensitivity to events:** Analytical skills: Self-knowledge: Ability to learn

The value of reflecting upon your own behaviour is an underlying theme in this book. Do this in a purposeful, insightful manner and you will get better at tuning in to situations and learning from experiences. You will develop greater self-awareness and the ability to cope with pressure and emotions.

A *personal journal* is based on the old idea of keeping some form of diary. However, this personal journal is structured around a model of human behaviour. To get the best value from it, you need to keep the journal over at least a few weeks.

In this model, there are three aspects of human behaviour:

1. *FEELINGS*: the way we act is partly determined by our feelings in a given situation. We are often unaware or only partly aware of our feelings and the effect they are having on our behaviour. There is often a learned tendency to suppress or deny feelings and to keep 'a stiff upper lip' – but if you are to be in control of your actions, it is essential to be sensitive to your feelings and their effects.

2. *THOUGHTS AND IDEAS*: in any situation we have a number of thoughts and ideas about what is going on and what we might do about it. These thoughts will depend on the various elements present and by our own assumptions and the perceptions brought in from previous experiences. Also important are any new ideas triggered by the new situation.

3. *ACTION-TENDENCIES*: we also have various action-tendencies. Action-tendencies are internal motivations or predispositions that push individuals towards certain types of action or inaction. For example, although disagreeing strongly with someone in a meeting, I might not say anything because I don't like challenging authority. This fear or lack of confidence leads to an action-tendency of saying/doing nothing. Another action-tendency could be a strong need to *do* something, to be impulsive rather than think things out carefully.

These three elements combine to influence our behaviour. In the example above of strong disagreement with the views of a leader: my *thoughts/ideas* are that what has been said is wrong; as a result, my *feelings* are those of concern and excitement; however, owing to my other *feeling* of fear of challenging authority, my *action-tendency* is to say and do nothing.

My behaviour in this situation will depend on which of the three elements wins out. These three elements also affect each other, so that my thoughts about what is being said often depend on my feelings about the person saying it – and vice versa. Figure A8.1 shows the links between thoughts/ideas, feelings and action-tendencies.

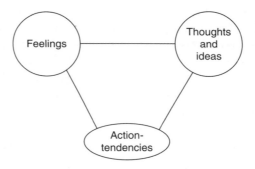

Figure A8.1 Links between thoughts/ideas, feelings and action-tendencies

Although this model of behaviour is simple, the situations in which it operates are often very complicated. Feelings, thoughts/ideas and action-tendencies don't exist in a vacuum but arise in response to situational stimuli (themselves affected by previous events) and they result in behaviour, which leads to a new situation, and so on (see Figure A8.2).

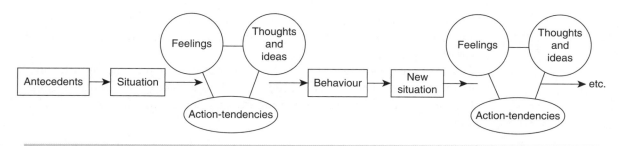

Figure A8.2 *The effect situational stimuli have on thoughts/ideas, feelings and action-tendencies*

Activity

Keep the personal journal going for a minimum of 20 entries, with at least four entries each week. A single entry might cover one specific incident, or may deal with a whole day's activities.

Some people find the personal journal so useful that it becomes part of their way of life. If you keep it up for a few weeks, you will find that you are beginning to develop a 'mental' personal journal as a way of thinking.

Step 1

Take an exercise book and mark left- and right-hand pages as shown in Table A8.1. If you want more space under any heading, continue overleaf.

Table A8.1   **Events and responses**

What happened	My responses
	My feelings
	My thoughts and ideas
	My action-tendencies
	Hence … My behaviour

On the left-hand page write a brief description of any event that impacts on you at work. This should be factual and objective, and include a description of what led up to the situation.

Write your responses to the situation on the right-hand page. Your feelings might have changed during the event. Identify and note these. Identify feelings that were closely followed by different ones, e.g. anger often follows a feeling of being threatened.

- Note the thoughts that you had during the situation; identify facts and assumptions.
- Then note your action-tendencies. What other factors influenced your action (or non-action)? How did your feelings, thoughts and action-tendencies affect each other?
- Finally, note the effect of these elements on your behaviour – what did you actually do?

Step 2

After seven or eight entries, you can take the journal further by adding another heading, *Learning*, to Table A8.1. Record your learning from these events and from your feelings, thoughts/ideas, action-tendencies and behaviour.

Looking back over your previous journal entries. Do you see any emerging patterns that tell you anything significant about yourself and other people?

Step 3

NOW WHAT?

How will you use these new insights and learning? How will you change your behaviour as a result?

Compile the journal over a period of time and you will become more insightful about situations and your actions in them, and you will also learn how to learn from everyday experience.

Follow-up

Should you become keen on the idea of 'journaling', the first thing to do is to buy yourself an attractive blank notebook from a bookstore and start writing. Alternatively, there are a number of software programs that provide free trial versions to test out whether they are for you. Try, for example: www.lifejournal.com, www.splinterware.com/products/idailydiary.htm or www.davidrm.com.

Many texts are available on journaling for all aspects of personal development, including health, spiritual awareness and gardening! If you'd like to step away from relying purely on writing in a journal, you may find that Linda Woods and Karen Dinino's *Journal Revolution: Rise Up & Create Art Journals, Personal Manifestos & Other Artistic Insurrections* (North Light Books, 2007) opens up whole new worlds of activity for you including writing on walls.

Use Your Power

Managerial qualities	**Sensitivity to events:** People skills: Initiative

If the road to hell is paved with good intentions, then efforts to change things often founder on the rocks of the power dynamics of organizations. We complain about 'politics' and about things happening for political reasons. The implication is that influence has been exerted and strings pulled – often in private – in a way that defeats the rational or common-sense way forward.

Many of us feel wary about power, its uses and abuses. This starts at home and school and carries on into the world of work. Perhaps we have suffered from others abusing their power over us, and we have all used our own power in an abusive way at some time or another. Yet very little can be done without power; indeed, it is just as frequently used in a good way – to protect the weak, to influence the unwise, to achieve valued ends. Power is inherent in all situations and in all relationships. In order that it should not corrupt us, we need to understand it, how it works and how it works in us.

All organizations are political systems and all leaders and managers are political actors engaged in the 'art of the possible'. All need awareness, understanding and the ability to act effectively in this political world. This activity will help you think through the different kinds of power and the various patterns of power relationships around you.

Sources of power in organizations

Power is a loose, hard-to-define term that includes personal attributes, resources, influences and authority. Here are some sources of power, but this list is not exhaustive, so you might like to add some categories of your own:

1. *Positional* – formal, hierarchical and status-related; position power exists when one person is 'higher' than another in a structure. Such power may carry outward signs or trappings such as expensive clothes, high salaries and designated parking spaces.
2. *Resources and rewards* – control of finance and other valued resources, access to premises and equipment and, in particular, to people and information are often crucial in getting things done.
3. *Knowledge and expertise* – possessing technical ability or professional knowledge, such as that of accountants, maintenance engineers, chemists, doctors, lawyers and computer engineers, is increasingly vital in this 'information age'. As with resource power, such power is easily withheld and is often used by professionals to counter positional power.
4. *Personal influence* – including track record and prior achievements. Personal influence is exercised in many ways, through interpersonal skills, persuasiveness, plausibility, charm, sexual attractiveness, intellectual weight or the capacity to inspire confidence and build trust.
5. *Networks and gossip* – within internal and external networks. 'Soft' gossipy information is often vital in terms of goings-on in the organization or the outside world. Some companies run 'soft information sessions' that link with developing environmental sensitivity and cultural awareness. The dark side of gossip is also well understood – for example, where knowledge of someone's personal life is used to damage them – but the importance of the light side is less well recognized.
6. *Energy and stamina* – two important qualities in getting things done. Many 'great leaders' have these. Staying power through stamina, adaptability, survival skills, occasional courage, steadfastness, standing by colleagues, and persistence without becoming obsessive is often underestimated, but frequently triumphs.

Activity

Use the matrix in Table A9.1 to see where the power lies in your organization – and where you stand in relation to the various kinds of power.

Table A9.1   **Powerlines matrix**

People / Sources of power	Me	My boss	My people	Colleagues	etc.
Positional					
Resources and rewards					
Knowledge and expertise					
Personal influence					
Networks and gossip					
Energy and stamina					
(Add your own)					

Step 1

Think about the kinds of power outlined above and add any others which you think we have missed or which carry special importance where you work.

Step 2

Choose a current issue or project that you are thinking about or working on. It might be the chance of you being chosen to lead a particular new scheme, or it might be the general influence of your department compared with others. It will help your analysis of the situation if you think about power in relation to something specific.

Now, using Table A9.1 score yourself or your department on each type of power, using the following scale:

5 = Very strong – well placed to deal with challenge/change/competition
4 = Strong – able to respond to new developments
3 = Adequate – will get by with a fair wind and stable conditions
2 = Weak – not well placed to cope with new developments
1 = Very weak – unable to cope with what's happening
0 = Desperate!

Now use the same scoring system to assess the power of the other important people or groups of people in your organization. We have listed your boss, staff, colleagues, etc., but you can customize this matrix for your own purposes. For example, if you were thinking about your chances of leading a particular project, you might include the other candidates; if you were thinking about the general influence of your department, you would include yours and all the other departments.

Step 3

Total the scores in *each vertical column* (for the matrix as it stands above, without any additional factors that you may have put in). The maximum total possible for each vertical column is $6 \times 5 = 30$. Looking at the figures, ask yourself the following questions:

◼ Is it obvious where the power lies?

_____

_____

_____

◼ Are there marked disparities of power between people or groups?

_____

_____

_____

◼ Am I making best use of my strengths?

_____

_____

_____

◼ How can I build up my weak areas of power?

_____

_____

_____

Now total the scores *across the columns* for each factor, and compare these with the possible totals in each direction. Ask yourself the following questions:

■ Is there a particular source of power in play here?

_____

_____

_____

■ How do I stand on that type?

_____

_____

_____

■ Is there a particularly under-used source of power here that I can bring into play?

_____

_____

_____

Step 4

Finally, create an action plan for yourself to build up your weak areas of power. You can use Activity 41, *Action Planning*, for this.

What you can do here depends on the resources you have available. Some sorts of power (e.g. connection power) may be easier to acquire than others – just get out more! Position power and rewards and punishment are less easy to acquire.

A good idea is to observe and then get to meet other people in your business that you view as powerful. Why do you see them in this way? Do they see themselves like this? What is the source of their power? Talk to them about it – people are often happy to talk about their strengths.

Power has fascinated us for millennia, and continues to do so. Analysing your situation, as a leader and manager through the activities in this book, is a simple way of doing this and may help you to use your powers more wisely. This comes partly through understanding better and also perhaps by seeing one or two things that you could do to help.

Follow-up

Other Activities in this book that will help you with ideas about how to build your power are Activities 11 (*Political Awareness*), 43 (*Managing Upwards*) and 52 (*Managing Your Dependency*).

Power is one of the core practices of leadership described especially in Chapter 7 of our *A Manager's Guide to Leadership* (McGraw-Hill, 2nd edition, 2010). Andrew Sobel and Jerold Panas's *Power Questions: Build Relationships, Win New Business, and Influence Others* (Wiley, 2012) is an interesting approach that makes questions the key to using your power – no less than 337 of them!

A collective view of power is taken by Diana Whitney and Amanda Trosten-Bloom in *The Power of Appreciative Enquiry: A Practical Guide to Positive Change* (Berrett-Koehler, 2010). Though indeed relentlessly positive, this book has the interesting perspective that power resides in a collaborative approach to getting things done.

Differences and Discrimination

Managerial qualities	**Sensitivity to events:** Professional knowledge and skills: Situational facts

The six jobs or achievements listed below on the left are those of six people listed on the right – but they have been jumbled up. Can you match them up correctly?

Job achievement

A. Orchestral musician

B. Embroidery designer

C. Steeplejack

D. Pilot

E. Front office receptionist for catering/tourism training organization

F. Winner of Whitbread literature prize

Person

1. 15-year-old with cerebral palsy

2. Woman with serious physical disability who is 3'11" tall

3. Profoundly deaf person

4. 55-year-old housewife

5. Person with two artificial legs

6. Colour-blind man

The correct answers are given at the end of this activity, but the main purpose here is for you to reflect on your reactions to the task – what went through your mind as you thought about the matching task?

Reflections of this kind can yield a lot of insight into how easily we all use preconceived notions and stereotypes to discriminate amongst and against people. Discrimination is a measure of good judgement – and weighing people up and their qualities is part of this. However, we can also make mistakes and discriminate against people on irrelevant and illegitimate grounds such as gender, sexual orientation, social class, skin colour, age, disability, religion and so on, at personal cost to them but often also at great loss to organizations. Good organizations have policies to ensure fairness and equal opportunity, but it is easy to get these things wrong when they are unfamiliar.

We have laws against certain types of discrimination, victimization and harassment, but many people are unaware that both *direct* and *indirect* discrimination are illegal. Direct discrimination means treating a person or group less favourably on gender or racial grounds than others would be treated in similar circumstances; indirect discrimination refers to unjustifiable requirements or conditions that may look equitable, but are not because particular groups can't comply with them.

Recruitment and selection are an area that worries many managers because of the costs of getting it wrong. Nothing in the law prevents an employer from choosing the best person for a job, so long as there is no discrimination because of sex, marital status or race. The activity below offers a framework to help you avoid discriminatory or exclusionary practices.

Activity

A person specification (or job specification) is the first step in a careful approach to recruitment and selection. This is created from a job description and describes the qualities needed to do the job satisfactorily under (a) essential and (b) desirable; it can also be helpful to list (c) contraindicators – things that genuinely disqualify someone for the work. A person specification does not guarantee good selection, but it can greatly reduce errors. One of the best known formats for the person specification is the 'Seven-Point Plan' (Table A10.1).

Step 1

Specifications can become biased in subtle ways, such as via fallacies that may be unconscious, that certain types of work are 'more suitable' for men or women. With senior jobs, factors of social class and status can become

Table A10.1 The Seven-Point Plan person specification

	Essential	Desirable	Contraindicators
1. *Physical appearance* – what does the work demand in terms of general health, physical strength or stamina, eyesight, hearing, speech, appearance?			
2. *Attainments* – education, training, experience, achievements			
3. *General intelligence* – specific indicators of reasoning ability and learning capacity			
4. *Special aptitudes* (e.g. mechanical, manipulative, mathematical, verbal/written expression, creativity)			
5. *Interests* (e.g. intellectual, practical, active, social interests relevant to work)			
6. *Disposition* – requirements in terms of working alone, getting on with others, using initiative, accepting responsibility, influencing, working under pressure			
7. *Circumstances* (e.g. travel from home, availability at certain times)			

converted into standards of appearance, education or social interests. To see how a person specification can be influenced in this way, try the following exercise:

Thinking of most of the *managerial and leadership* jobs in your organization, how likely are recruitment and selection to discriminate, openly or indirectly, against some categories of people by:

- gender?
- marital status?
- age?
- skin colour?
- social class?
- disability?

Put your views in Table A10.2. Consider whether discrimination in recruitment and selection is likely to operate at leadership and managerial levels with regard to gender, then marital status, etc., for each of the factors in the

Table A10.2 **Possible discriminatory factors**

	Gender	Marital status	Age	Skin colour	Social class	Disability
1. Physical appearance						
2. Attainments						
3. General intelligence						
4. Special aptitudes						
5. Interests						
6. Disposition						
7. Circumstances						

Seven-Point Plan. If you think discrimination is likely to arise, put an ' × ' in the box. Otherwise, leave it blank or put in a question mark.

Step 2

For each area of discrimination you have identified:

■ Who is likely to be discriminated against?

_____

_____

_____

■ How is it likely to arise?

_____

_____

_____

■ How can it be avoided?

_____

_____

_____

Step 3

In relation to your current sphere of influence, do you think discrimination affects any aspect of work? If so, what could be done to eliminate it?

This aspect of relationships at work may lead to difficult personal or organizational questions. But it is bigger than just about avoiding discrimination – important though that is. Learning organizations wish to make the most of all the people and their learning and a company that is discriminatory is also likely to be ineffective in terms of making the most of its resourceful humans.

Follow-up

There are many sources of useful reading and information in this area, often specific to particular disabilities or areas of employment. The CIPD (Chartered Institute of Personnel and Development) might be a good place to start (www.cipd.co.uk). The CIPD publishes factsheets, guides and tools on various aspects of diversity.

Other useful contacts include:

(i)　Royal Association for Disability and Rehabilitation (RADAR): www.radar.org.uk
(ii)　Royal National Institute for the Blind (RNIB): www.rnib.org.uk
(iii)　Royal Association for Deaf People (RAD): www.royaldeaf.org.uk
(iv)　Equality and Human Rights Commission (EHRC): www.eoc.org.uk

For a readable, academic take on the topic, Gill Kirton and Anne-Marie Greene's *The Dynamics of Managing Diversity: A Critical Approach* (Butterworth-Heinemann, 2nd edition, 2010) is a well-established text.

Answers to matching task

A = 3 (Evelyn Glennie)
B = 6*
C = 4*
D = 5 (Sir Douglas Bader)
E = 2*
F = 1 (Christy Nolan, *Damburst of Dreams*)
* Private individuals known to the authors.

Political Awareness

Managerial qualities	**Sensitivity to events:** People skills: Initiative

Leaders and managers are increasingly expected to be politically sensitive and aware. We have lots of words to describe this ability – we call it *nous* or being *streetwise, savvy, clued-up, on the ball* – and recognize it in people who somehow know who to talk to, who to agree with and who to disagree with. We also recognize the political innocents among us who seem to have very little idea of what is going on. However knowledgeable or skilled you are in your own field, you can't get things done without knowing how the organization works.

Another problem is how to act with political awareness *and* with integrity. Many people enjoy some game-playing as part of the fun of being in the organization. But those for whom the game becomes the main issue we might call clever, but never wise. While innocents can exhibit a kind of wisdom, we would only use the word wise of someone who (a) knows what is going on; and (b) bases their actions on the longer-term perspective based on personal values rather than short-term political advantage.

This activity does not guarantee wisdom, but it might help you to become a little more streetwise around your organization.

Activity

Step 1

First, think of a change that you want to make – small or large. Even small changes – such as in paperwork systems, furniture layout, meal times and so on – will illustrate the effects of power and politics very nicely. However, make sure the change is important to you and that you do intend to make it.

Step 2

(i) Using the *Micro-political mapping: Who's who?* worksheet in Table A11.1, list in the left-hand column all the people and groups who are involved in making the change or who will be affected by it.

Table A11.1 **Micro-political mapping: Who's who?**

People/group	Interests	Power sources

(ii) Now list the *interests* of each of these people or groups in the middle column. When thinking of interests it is useful to consider:
- *vested* interests – salary, resources, career prospects, territory, advantages, perks, etc.
- *ideological* interests – political or philosophical commitments
- *self*-interests – personal values, sense of personal and professional identity.

(iii) Third, note in the right-hand column what you see as each person or group's main sources of power. One classification of power sources is as follows:
1. position
2. resources and rewards
3. knowledge and expertise
4. personal influence

5. networks and gossip
6. energy and stamina.

(You will find explanations of these in Activity 9, *Use Your Power*.)

Having listed all those involved, their interests and sources of power, to which of these do you need to pay special attention?

If you have a long list, you may feel that it would be better to let sleeping dogs lie. A well-known problem with analysis is that it can lead to paralysis. However, that is not the intention here: the aim is to empower you to act with political awareness and integrity! The next step should help you to move on.

Step 3

Now consider the *orientation* of each of your people or groups to the change you have in mind. The worksheet in Table A11.2 has two dimensions:

(i) *Support/resist* – is the person or group supportive of or resistant to the change?
(ii) *Power* – does the person or group have high or low power in this situation?

Table A11.2 **Micro-political mapping: change orientation**

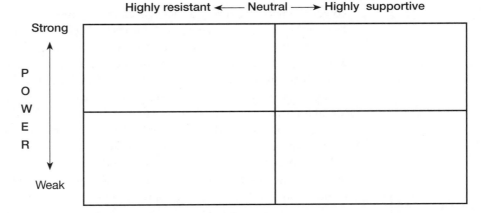

This gives four obvious locations:

Powerful and supportive	Powerful and resistant
Weak and supportive	Weak and resistant

Now mark your people or groups on the worksheet. You can assign them simply to one of the quadrants or you can grade them carefully with regard to the vertical and horizontal scales.

Step 4

How does your chart look? Does it show a critical mass of support for your change or solid ranks of resistance against it?

In the latter case, should you rethink your ideas or reconsider your plans?

If, as often, the picture is more evenly balanced, what could you do to increase support for your change? Can you approach individuals or groups to:

■ Find out why the resisters are resisting? Do they understand fully the proposed change? What are their objections? Is there anything they would like which would change their positions?

■ Ask powerful supporters to approach powerful resisters to try to 'get them on board' or at least to reduce their resistance?

■ Help those who are supportive but weak become more powerful. Perhaps the people in this quadrant could be brought together to reduce isolation and develop a sense of joint identity. Can they be encouraged to speak up at meetings? Can their status be raised in any way?

Follow-up

Power is one of the core practices of leadership described in Chapter 5 of our *A Manager's Guide to Leadership* (McGraw-Hill, 2nd edition, 2010).

There are lots of materials on the web including YouTube videos, one of which is a 45-minute lecture on the hidden secrets of power and influence at work: http://www.youtube.com/watch?v = b9DL5TLow3E.

If you are looking for a book that gives the topic a popular treatment suitable for managerial situations, then *How to Influence: The Art of Making Things Happen* by Jo Owen (Prentice-Hall, 2010) explores the art of making things happen through other people and is full of ideas.

Some people find it hard to understand why thinking about power is useful in preparing to make changes. Niccolò Machiavelli is often invoked with his ruminations on 'whether it is better to be loved than to be feared' and his exhortation to 'be like a lion and a fox' (presumably, to be able to be forthright and honest as well as sly and devious). Some organizations do bear a passing resemblance to the Medici Court, and if you happen to work in one of these then perhaps *The Prince* is still as good a guide as any – or if you prefer an updated equivalent, try Jonathan Powell's *The New Machiavelli: How to Wield Power in the Modern World* (Vintage Books, 2010). Powell was Tony Blair's chief-of-staff for ten years, so he will have had many opportunities to observe such behaviours.

Credulous Listening

Managerial qualities	**Sensitivity to events:** People skills: Ability to learn

If you want to know something about a person, ask – they just might tell you.

George Kelly

George Kelly published his ideas almost 50 years ago, and the implications are still emerging. Kelly believed that although the world is real and not a figment of our imaginations, each individual tries for him or herself to grasp and make sense of the world and only ever partly succeeds. We all construct our own understandings or *personal constructs*, which are each person's unique ways of understanding his or her world. We have common understandings with others, but only if we have a sense of their value systems as well as our own.

In working with people, Kelly places great importance on *credulous listening*, which involves:

(i) believing that what the other person says is true for them; and
(ii) suspending our own ideas and constructs in order to understand the *personal constructs* of the other person.

This can be difficult. In talking with others, we may often internally translate what they are saying so that it matches our own ideas. Sometimes our own ideas, prejudices and assumptions get in the way so much that we think, 'Why is she telling me this?' or 'Here he goes again!', so that we hardly hear what they say at all. To deal with this problem, it is necessary to become – at least for a time – a *credulous listener*.

Activity

Step 1

Choose a time when you know that you are going to be meeting with someone whose ideas, values or beliefs you find difficult to agree with.

Decide that you will listen credulously to everything that they are going to say – yes, everything!

This means that you will be accepting that what they say is *true for them*.

Step 2

Because credulous listening is difficult, set yourself a target, say, to listen credulously for 20 or 30 minutes. If possible, take a break at this point to jot down their ideas and perhaps to reflect them back to the person. Take the chance to check whether you have fully understood the meanings and implications that the words have for the other person.

To listen credulously to another, you also have to listen to yourself. When you 'hear' yourself becoming incredulous, and in order to suspend these views, say to yourself something like: 'What this person is saying is true for them, I don't have to agree or disagree, but just listen and try to understand.'

If you do any interviewing or counselling you will have had a taste of this experience. Here the task is to enable the other person to portray *their* point of view, *their* taste, *their* perceptions. Yet, even in this formal situation, it can be very hard not to impose your own construction of events on what is being said, and reveal this in your tone of voice, raised eyebrows, selective questions and so on.

Step 3

- How did you do?
- Did you really listen credulously?
- Do you understand that person's view of the world better?

If you can answer 'Yes' to the above questions, then give yourself a pat on the back. You have given another person that all too rare experience of being really listened to, and you might well have learned something new for yourself. Through credulous listening we escape the limits of our own thoughts and imaginations and gain access to a wider world.

Practising credulous listening is one of the most valuable skills that you are likely to find in this book. You can practise this on your own by doing some *credulous reading*. This involves the two processes – loosening and

tightening – that Kelly made central to his idea of people as experimenters continually testing their understandings of the world. Loosening (exploring and trying out ideas) and tightening (choosing options and making things happen) are reciprocal and repeated activities that are core to the learning process.

Next time you're reading a book, think about the *way* you're reading. Here are two possible extreme positions:

'Being taken over' by the story, being enamoured, getting lost in it (loosening)		'Reading for a purpose', ransacking the text for a specific end; instrumental; judgemental (tightening)

Depending on *how* you read it, you will take different things from the book. It's the same as with people.

Follow-up

Trevor Butt's *George Kelly: The Psychology of Personal Constructs* (Palgrave Macmillan, 2008) is a readable text covering the development of Kelly's work and showing how it can be used in a variety of settings.

The Centre for Personal Construct Psychology at the University of Hertfordshire (http://www.centrepcp.co.uk) has introductory accounts of PCP and offers a variety of learning programmes including on-line versions. It also has a useful library with books on the application of PCP to counselling, education, clinical practice and other specialisms.

Decision Making

Managerial qualities	**Analytical skills**

Making decisions is a critical aspect of the leader or manager's job. Robert Townsend said that perhaps 40% of the decisions he made as CEO of Avis turned out to be wrong. The important thing, he said, was that he made them.

So, a first-class leader might average 50% or 60% correct decisions. (It takes a first-class leader to admit this.) All decisions are hedged with uncertainty – otherwise they would not be decisions – yet we humans have a remarkable facility for 'rationalizing' and justifying our actions, and do this for ourselves even when not called to account by others. If we did less of this we would recognize how many of our decisions turned out to be wrong, and therefore be prepared accordingly. An initial decision on a new project can spawn many more crisis/decision points as it gets under way.

Broadly speaking, there are two ways of making decisions:

- ◼ A 'rational' process of planning: specifying alternatives, criteria and payoff probabilities until the 'correct' solution emerges (Type A).
- ◼ Following 'hunches' or intuition: taking action without planning because action creates information and information reduces uncertainty (Type B).

Depending on our training and personality, most of us use one of these modes more than the other – even to the exclusion of the other. This is perhaps natural, but it limits our capacity for meeting different kinds of decisions. Complex decisions may demand the use of both modes at different times.

Activity

Below are some sample decisions. Although some may be complex, we shall treat them as simple and say that one mode of decision making is more suitable than the other.

Step 1

Read each sample decision and decide whether it is Type A (rational) or Type B (intuitive):

1. Getting yourself from your place of work to a meeting in another specific location.
2. Being dropped anywhere in the country, without knowing where, with £10, and the task of getting home. Imagine yourself standing in open country surrounded by a light fog.
3. Choosing the means of communicating some minor redundancies in the company, given a 48-hour deadline and a partly unionized workforce.
4. Selecting an incentive payment scheme for a work area where workloads are extremely variable and where payment has previously been on a flat rate.
5. Deciding how to approach your boss about a favour you want and knowing that he or she can be very moody and changeable.
6. Deciding how to run a particular appraisal interview.

You might well say that you would use both decision types as appropriate. We say that, in *broad terms*, the decisions split as shown in Table A14.1.

Table A14.1 A = rational; B = intuitive

Decision	Type
1	A
2	B
3	A
4	A
5	B
6	B

Step 2

Your choice of decision type has a very marked effect on how you act when faced with a particular problem. Think about and jot down the steps you would take on Decisions 1 and 2 above. Then answer the following:

(a) Are your notes very similar for Decisions 1 and 2, or very different?

_____

_____

(b) Which did you find easier: Decision 1 or 2?

_____

_____

You probably found Decision 1 easier to tackle.

Decision 1 is Type A (rational) – the goal is clear and there are relatively well-structured alternatives. Therefore, a rational decision is possible by sifting the alternatives against the criteria and choosing appropriately as in Table A14.2.

Decision 2 does not lend itself to such an analysis. There is a clear goal: you want to get home, but you have no idea where you are and there is much more uncertainty in this situation than in Decision 1, with no clearly structured alternative actions open to you.

With this lack of information, the value of planning is limited. In well-structured situations, *planning* can usefully precede *action*; in unstructured situations, where uncertainty predominates, it is better to act quickly because *action generates information*. In conditions of uncertainty, *action has to precede planning*, because it generates the information required for planning. Or, to put it another way, the first objective in uncertain situations is to generate information. You choose an action to this end and pursue it until further information is obtained, at which point planning may be appropriate.

In Decision 2, an intelligent action is to walk in a fixed direction (not in a circle) because this would give you maximum chance of uncovering information: a stream, a path, a road, a clearing in the mist, etc. If you find a path, you clearly have a much more structured choice – whether to follow it and in which direction. As paths always lead from one place to another, you will tend to follow it in the hope of finding out where you are, i.e. to generate more information. Eventually, you will generate enough information to know what kind of a problem you have in getting home, and what the alternatives are. You are then back in a rational decision 1 process.

Table A14.2

Problem-solving stages	Decision 1
1. Analyse the problem in terms of: (a) how things are (b) how I want things to be	1. I am at work and I want to get to the meeting in London
2. Specify *your objective* in terms of the change you want to bring about (i.e. A → B)	2. (Already stated in 1 above)
3. Specify the *alternative courses of action* open to you to achieve the objective	3. Go by: – car – train – taxi – bus – plane – get a lift from a colleague
4. Specify the *criteria* (i.e. what characteristics a course of action must have to achieve your objective)	4. (i) I need to be there by 10 a.m. and I don't want to stay overnight (before or after) (ii) It must not cost more than £50 (iii) It would be useful to be able to read the papers for the meeting on the journey (iv) I need to be fresh on arrival
5. Choose the alternative that best meets the criteria	5. The train meets the criteria. The car fails on criteria (iii) and (iv); the bus is noisy and fails on criterion (iv); there is no plane until 10 a.m. and it fails on criterion (i); travelling with a colleague is possible but would hinder criterion (iii)
6. Implement the alternative	6. Catch the train
7. Check whether you have achieved your goal; if not, return to 1	7. Did you get to the meeting fresh and on time?

In Decision 5 there are no obvious alternative courses of action because the boss is *unpredictable*. A carefully planned strategy could be disastrous because plans possess momentum that is hard to modify. The best approach might be to stay neutral until your boss's behaviour provides clues to their mood, then you can plan on your feet what action to take.

Decision 6 is a similar situation unless you regard it as a one-way process – in which case you can adopt a 'rational' approach without the need to generate information about the other person's feelings and views. Yet most interpersonal situations demand the *action before planning* approach and this is the area of decision making that creates many problems for managers. Those who are able

to suspend their planning skills to generate sufficient information about alternatives and criteria *according to other people* will usually make better decisions. They are more 'socially skilled' than managers who impose a previously planned 'rational' decision upon others.

To summarize: use a rational process for well-structured situations and an *action before planning* approach where there is little or no information (you must first be able to admit/recognize that there is little or no information). In uncertain situations, the following advice is useful:

- Regard obtaining information as an objective in itself.
- Be prepared to get quickly into action of a kind that generates information.
- Be prepared to go through many cycles of action → information → planning → action.

This is also a rational decision-making process once you recognize its cyclical nature; the need to start with information-getting as the objective; the need to move into action on an experimental basis.

Step 3

As a final test of your understanding of the difference between the two approaches to decision making, reflect upon a recent or current decision and ask yourself:

- Has 'information-getting' been an objective?
- Has there been enough experimental action?
- Have I picked up all the information available from experimental action and from elsewhere?
- Have I analysed the available information carefully and did it result in improved understanding?

Follow-up

Mindtools is an excellent website (www.mindtools.com/pages/main/newMN_TED.htm) that offers 40 decision-making tools, including Critical Thinking, Pareto Analysis and the Kepner-Tregoe Technique. It explains what these tools are and shows how to use them.

Sheila Cottrell's *Critical Thinking Skills: Developing Effective Analysis and Argument* (Palgrave Macmillan, 2011) is the second edition of a bestselling book, which is very thorough but also attractively laid out with checklists and figures. John Adair's *Decision Making and Problem Solving* (CIPD, 2010) is a practical introduction to techniques of decision making.

Planning and Decision Making

There are many planning and decision-making techniques, each with many variations. Opinions vary about their usefulness, a common criticism being that techniques work well on classroom-type examples designed to show how they work, but that they rarely fit neatly with the problems encountered by managers.

However, there are a number of basic techniques that any manager should know about. From a self-development standpoint there are plenty of resources available, especially on the web, and large organizations will have specialists who can advise. Here we provide an activity to check and extend your awareness of some core techniques. If any of these seems pertinent to your situation, the Follow-up resources will help you proceed further.

A point about management techniques in general. For any given technique, certain individuals will have *specialized* in this area and devoted much work to it. They will have developed variations and refinements of the basic techniques, and entered into complex debate with each other about them. They will have been most interested in complex and ambitious applications, often involving project teams working over many months.

Against this background we make two claims that you might like to consider (particular experts might disagree!):

■ The *core idea* in each technique is relatively simple (as are most good ideas) and easily grasped by a normal, intelligent person.

■ Application of any technique can be brief. You can learn a good technique in 15 minutes on the back of an envelope. Once the idea of each technique has been grasped, it should be possible to incorporate the key ideas and principles into your thinking, and apply the technique 'inside your head'. So the main pay-off from studying these methods may be in the general effect they have on how you think, rather than through the formal and explicit application of the techniques.

Activity

Step 1

Look at the list of techniques/methods below. Do they mean anything to you? Write under each what you know about them.

■ Critical path analysis/network planning.

_____

_____

■ Value analysis.

_____

_____

■ Linear programming.

_____

_____

■ Break-even-point analysis.

_____

_____

■ Cost–benefit analysis.

_____

_____

■ Cost-effectiveness analysis.

_____

_____

■ Discounted cash flow.

_____

_____

Step 2

Compare your understanding with the brief descriptions below.

Critical path analysis/network planning

This is a method of planning for complex, often one-off projects like erecting a building, installing a new plant, or moving an operation from one location to another. In such operations, a series of tasks have to be performed in the right order and at the right time for the objective to be achieved on time.

The overall method is to list the tasks to be done, work out the order of priorities and draw a 'map' of operations, as in Figure A14.1 (although, of course, it will be much more complicated). The idea is that to do the whole job, one has to work down all the 'paths' from left to right. From here it is possible to plan time and resources for each task, and work out which sequence of operations, if delayed, would delay the whole project (this sequence is the 'critical path').

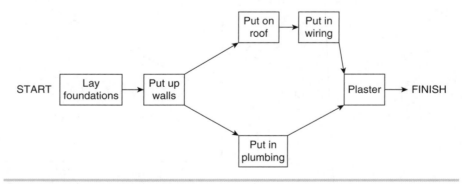

Figure A14.1 Critical path analysis/network planning

Value analysis

This is a process of taking something that is produced, at a cost, to perform a function (usually a product, but it can be a service) and analysing where the cost goes (parts, assembly tasks, etc.), assessing what these cost elements actually contribute to the performance of the product's function. On the basis of this, ways of reducing the cost of the product without impairing its ability to perform its function can be sought.

Linear programming

The linear-programming problem is exemplified by the farmer who has a choice of foodstuffs for his cattle, each at different prices, each with different proportions of, say, protein, fat and carbohydrate. The farmer knows what the cattle require in terms of minimum quantities of the three forms of food. The problem is to work out the cheapest combination of the available foodstuffs to meet these requirements.

Break-even-point analysis

What it costs to make most mass-produced goods can be split more or less into 'fixed' and 'variable' costs. Fixed costs are incurred once you have decided to set up facilities for production. Variable costs are those costs that increase in proportion to the number of items you make. In car manufacture, setting up a production line is a fixed cost, whereas the materials and labour that go into making the cars are a variable cost, because for each extra car you produce the more you need of them. The cost of producing various numbers of products can therefore be shown on a graph (see Figure A14.2).

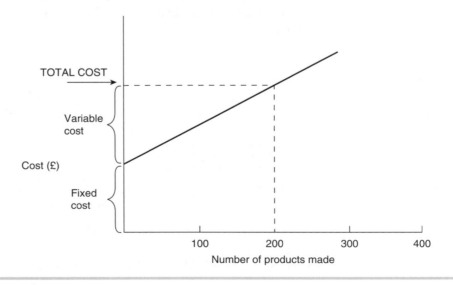

Figure A14.2

Another graph can be drawn (Figure A14.3) relating revenue to the number of products sold.

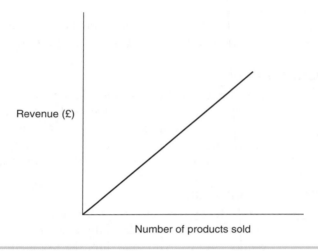

Revenue (£)

Number of products sold

Figure A14.3

The slope of the line is determined by the price. The two graphs can be superimposed (Figure A14.4).

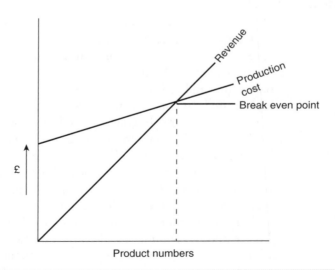

Revenue

Production cost

Break even point

£

Product numbers

Figure A14.4

The break-even point is where the two lines meet. At this point, revenue from sales equals production cost and you have 'broken even'. Make and sell more than that and you have a financial return. Make and sell less and you are making a loss.

This kind of analysis is particularly relevant to pricing decisions, and deciding whether it is worth going into a certain line of business.

Cost–benefit analysis

Cost–benefit analysis is simply looking at a decision in terms of what it would *cost* to go for each alternative, and what the benefit would be from pursuing each alternative in cost terms (e.g. a transport firm might evaluate different makes and sizes of lorries for its fleet in terms of purchase cost, maintenance costs and running costs against the return it would get over the lorries' lives).

Cost-effectiveness analysis

Cost-effectiveness analysis is intended for situations in which it is difficult to quantify the benefit side of the equation. It starts from the point of assuming that one wants to do something, looks for alternatives that are equally effective in doing it, and chooses the cheapest (e.g. a firm may decide that it must provide its employees with a canteen affording a given level of service at given hours, and at a given meal price). It then looks at alternative ways of doing this (e.g. hiring a catering contractor or taking on staff), works out what the alternatives cost and makes a choice.

Discounted cash flow

Many business decisions involve choosing a line of action that entails making expenditures at different points of time in the future, in the hope of generating revenue at other points of time in the future. Thus, flowing out of a transport business there is the initial cost of vehicles, and the further costs of maintenance, fuel and drivers' wages spread over the life of the vehicles, plus expenditure on replacing mechanical parts, etc.; flowing in should be a steady stream of revenue from freight charges paid by customers. A decision like this involves working out if by going in for this enterprise one would end up better off, and better off by enough to make it worth the trouble.

Because £100 now is not worth the same as the promise of £100 in one year's time, it is not enough to calculate expected cash flow out (costs) and in (revenue). Discounted cash flow allows for this by correcting expected costs and revenues at different times to their value at the same time (usually now). This is done by assuming a discount rate (which might be the interest rate at which money can be borrowed, or an estimate of inflation or a rate fixed by the organization for the purpose) and using this to 'correct' the value of revenues and costs.

If a rate of 5% is assumed (as an estimate of likely inflation, or because this is the cost of borrowing money to finance the project), the £100 would be worth £105 in one year's time. Cost or revenue of £100 in one year's time would be counted as £95.24 now. Thus all costs and revenues of the project can be corrected to current-value equivalents to obtain a more accurate estimate of the value of the project.

1. Think carefully whether any of these techniques 'fit' any of your problems.
2. 'Do it yourself' on a specific problem, working out the way from the descriptions above.
3. Choose the techniques that interest you and follow them up with further reading and study.

Follow-up

If you want a substantial text, you'll find 468 pages on various techniques in *Decision Analysis for Management Judgment* by Paul Goodwin, George Wright and Lawrence Phillips (Wiley, 4th edition, 2009). On accounting specifically, the latest edition of Colin Drury's tried and tested *Management and Cost Accounting* (Cengage Learning EMEA, 8th edition, 2012) is useful.

You will also find plenty of web-based description and advice on these techniques. For example, MindTools has these and more besides under Project Management Skills (www.mindtools.com/pages/main/newMN_PPM.htm). And if you enter a specific technique into your search engine, it will throw up case examples of, for example, Value Analysis being applied to British Airways or Tesco.

Role Set Analysis

Managerial qualities	**Analytical skills:** Situational facts

The concept of role has a central place in organizational theories. Leadership roles, decision-making roles and supervisory roles are just a few examples of the frequent use we make of this term.

The term is borrowed from the stage where it is an act or a series of actions. In performing the life roles of child, wife or husband, parent or neighbour, while we remain ourselves, our behaviour is largely determined by the role we occupy at a given time. Indeed, if we don't alter behaviour appropriately in these situations, we run into trouble. Errors of this sort – as in speaking to your partner as you might to your young child – are a form of role conflict.

This conflict happens because all roles carry expectations about behaviour. Attached to each role are the other people who make up a role network. Role conflict occurs when:

- Two people make opposing or conflicting demands on the role-holder, e.g. the boss who wants the manager to discipline his staff who, in turn, want protection from the boss.
- We occupy several different roles in quick succession and the demands of one conflict with those of another, e.g. work roles conflict with partner and parent roles when you need to work late or at the weekend.
- Roles carry expectations that conflict with personal values, e.g. as a senior manager I have to overlook some commercial practices, such as giving inducements to secure certain contracts, which I disapprove of ethically.

Role conflict is a major cause of workplace stress, and to avoid stress, role relationships have to be managed like any other part of the job. This activity will help you to think about your role as a leader or manager and:

- clarify your position within your organization
- establish what demands and expectations are made of you
- identify possible and actual areas of role conflict which helps to reduce the stress
- lay the foundations for improving your performance – at work and at home.

Activity

Step 1

Take a large sheet of paper and draw a circle in the middle of it to represent the role you occupy at work. Label this circle, for example, 'Office Manager' (J. Brown). Next, draw smaller circles around the centre circle to represent all the 'significant others' in the role network of the office manager. These are all the people who make demands upon and have expectations about the role. In addition, the role has reciprocal expectations and makes demands upon them.

You can show the strength of particular links by making these roles nearer or further from the centre. Those people with whom you have daily contact probably make more demands and have more expectations of you than those you meet weekly. The role network for the office manager might look like Figure A15.1.

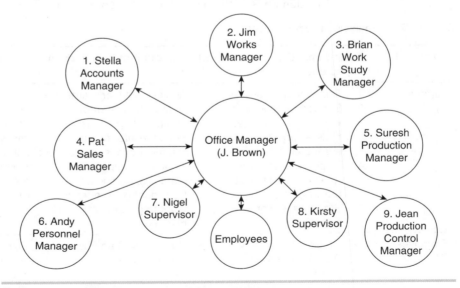

Figure A15.1   Role of network office manager

Step 2

Once you have completed your role network diagram, ask someone else their views about it.

■ Have you included all the significant role relationships?

_____

_____

■ How different is your role network from that of others around you?

_____

_____

■ How does it feel to be the 'person-in-the-middle' making and meeting all these demands?

_____

_____

Step 3

Once you have included all the vital role relationships for your job, take another sheet of paper and make a chart like that in Table A15.1. On the left-hand side put all those roles that make demands upon your role and fill in across the three columns: 'Their demands/expectations of me'; 'My expectations/demands of them'; and 'Possible conflict areas'.

Table A15.1   Analysis of expectations

Role	Their demands/ expectations of me	My expectations/demands of them	Possible conflict areas
Supervisors (2)	1. Fair allocation of work 2. Support for their actions 3. Personal support (e.g. to listen and be available) 4. To provide resources to allow them to get the work done 5. Set realistic work targets	1. Achieve set work targets 2. Deal with most grievances and people problems 3. Keep me informed about a variety of things (e.g. current workloads, supply of materials, personnel issues) 4. Be proactive – set own work targets in consultation with me	Supervisor actions, especially on discipline and grievances, are not always consistent with company personnel policy Supervisors dependent on me – will not take responsibility
Employees (16)	1. To treat them fairly 2. To arbitrate over matters of disagreement with supervisors	1. To work well and achieve work targets	Cannot satisfy both employees' demands on me to arbitrate *and* supervisors' demands for support of their actions
And so on ...			

Step 4

How can this role chart help?

■ First, are you aware of all the demands and expectations of you? Are you sure you have them right?
If you are in any doubt about what is expected of you by some other role holder, use this question to go and check this out.

■ Second, does your perception of what they want from you fit with theirs? If you asked them, would they agree with what you'd written?
Again, the obvious way to check this out is to ask – wherever you are in doubt.

■ Third, what conflicts appear – between different expectations, between you personally and your role demands, etc.?

How can you resolve or cope with these? Sometimes the answer is fairly simple. For example, on the office manager's role chart (Table A15.1), the first conflict area – 'Supervisor actions, especially on discipline and grievances, are not always consistent with company personnel policy' – may point to a training need.

Follow-up

The Wisdom of Teams: Creating the High-performance Organisation by Jon Katzenbach and Douglas Smith (McGraw-Hill, 2005) is a classic on this topic of team building. However, Peter Hawkins' *Leadership Team Coaching: Developing Collective Transformational Leadership* (Kogan Page, 2011) is a more recent and excellent book, defining what high performance looks like in teams and also giving you advice on how to coach teams to realize these qualities – or the five disciplines as he calls them.

Planning Change

Managerial qualities	**Analytical skills:** Initiative

This activity contains the famous planning tool *Force Field Analysis* and is credited to Kurt Lewin, whose 'field theory' described a field of forces or pressures acting on any particular event. In this view, all situations can be seen as being in temporary equilibrium, with the forces acting to change the situation being balanced by the forces acting to resist the change (Figure A16.1).

This view of events is a dynamic one, which sees all things, especially social situations, as temporary states of balance. It offers the leader the opportunity to see situations as potentially changeable: if the different forces can be identified, it may be possible to change their direction or strength.

Use this activity for a problem that has been worrying you and which seems intractable. The Force Field Analysis will make the options clearer and bring a vague problem into focus and be more 'do-able'.

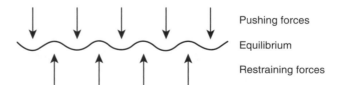

Figure A16.1 Force Field Analysis

Activity

Apply Force Field Analysis to a particular problem or situation which you currently face and which you would like to change or influence.

Step 1

Choose a problem and write it down.

It must be a real one that concerns you right now. The example given in Figure A16.2 is that of a manager worried by a rise in errors in their section.

Step 2

Define the problem in specific terms.

■   Who is involved?

_____

_____

■   What is the magnitude of the problem?

_____

_____

■   What other factors bear on the situation?

_____

_____

For example, errors have arisen in Section B over the last six months. Errors were averaging 5% but have now doubled to 10%. Relevant factors may include a recent influx of new staff and a change in incentives to increase output.

Step 3

Now state specifically how you would like to influence or change the situation.

Make this as measurable as possible; set a clear target and know when you are reaching it. For example, 'I aim to reduce the error rate to 6%'.

Step 4

Looking at the problem as a temporary equilibrium held in place (for the moment) by pushing and restraining forces, list these forces operating on your problem.

(a) What are the forces that would move the present situation towards my goal? (PUSHING FORCES)

(i) _____

_____

(ii) _____

_____

(iii) _____

_____

(iv) _____

_____

(v) _____

_____

(b) What are the forces resisting or stopping the situation approaching my goal? (RESTRAINING FORCES)

(i) _____

_____

(ii) _____

_____

(iii) _____

_____

       (iv)   _____

                _____

       (v)   _____

                _____

For example, on the problem of reducing Section B's error rate:

(a) PUSHING FORCES (to reduce error rate):
- (i)   manager's desire to lower the rate
- (ii)   company's concern at its image
- (iii) staff concern at loss of earnings
- (iv) customer complaints
- (v)   planned training courses for new staff.

(b) RESTRAINING FORCES (tending to increase error rate):
- (i)   influx of untrained staff
- (ii)   company pressure for increased output
- (iii) new incentive scheme
- (iv) casual attitude of younger staff concerning general behaviour and discipline
- (v)   resentment of some older staff at being pushed on output.

Make sure you have listed all the forces operating on the problem. Have you included in particular:

- ■ the motivations of individuals and groups involved?
- ■ organizational policies and procedures?
- ■ outside forces operating in the work environment?

Step 5

When you have all the relevant forces listed, rank their power as being HIGH, MEDIUM or LOW.
    Do this for both PUSHING and RESTRAINING FORCES.

Step 6

Now depict the two sets of forces as in the example in Figure A16.2, using the length of the arrows to indicate the magnitude of the force. In the example, the manager's desire to reduce the rate is a HIGH power PUSHING force, whereas the casual attitude of younger staff is a MEDIUM power RESTRAINING force.

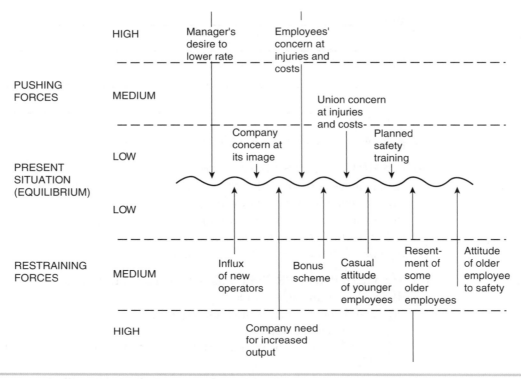

Figure A16.2 Force field analysis

Step 7

Now prepare a strategy for changing the situation.
Remember:

(a) *Increasing the PUSHING forces often creates **greater** resistance in people and in systems.*

(b) *Change is most easily accepted when it requires a minimum of effort and disruption.*

Can you:

1. Maintain PUSHING forces, but reduce any of the RESTRAINING forces?
2. Find new PUSHING forces?
3. If you must PUSH more, choose forces that do not increase resistance?
4. Divert any RESTRAINING forces to new targets or in new directions?

5. Ensure that it is not one of your PUSHING forces that created the problem in the first place? Would a reduction in this PUSH also reduce the RESTRAINING force?

Your strategy should plan some action steps in sequence, with rough timings and the resources you will need at each stage, particularly those people who can help.

It is very helpful to have sub-goals along the way to check your progress (a single far-off goal can be daunting). The lessons in Activity 13, *Decision Making*, about action creating information for further planning will also be useful here.

As an analysis tool, Force Field Analysis can be used to examine any problem situation. More than just a technique, it is a way of seeing situations as being only in temporary equilibrium and amenable to change.

Follow-up

There is a great deal about Force Field Analysis and other planning and change management tools on the web. For example, the NHS Institute for Innovation & Improvement has a good clear explanation at: http://www.institute.nhs.uk/ quality_and_service_improvement_tools/quality_and_service_improvement_ tools/force_field_analysis.html.

And the ubiquitous MindTools has another at: http://www.mindtools.com/ pages/article/newTED_06.htm.

Esther Cameron and Mike Green provide a good summary of Force Field Analysis (and many other techniques) in *Making Sense of Change Management: A Complete Guide to the Models, Tools and Techniques of Organizational Change* (Kogan Page, 3rd edition, 2012).

Catastrophic Contingencies

Managerial qualities	**Analytical skills:** Creativity: Emotional resilience: Initiative: Self-knowledge

Many leaders and managers, faced with complex decisions, find themselves blocked in by the fear of 'what if ...?' Faced with uncertainty, doubt and the possibility of a bad, even catastrophic, consequence of our action, we tend towards stress and the inability to act.

This activity is designed to help you overcome this kind of blockage.

Activity

Step 1

Next time you are faced with a difficult problem involving uncertainty, risk or doubt, first write down the various courses of action open to you. Then list the worst possible things that could happen if everything went wrong.

What are the worst catastrophes that could occur?

Step 2

Take each catastrophe in turn and imagine that it really has happened. How do you feel in this disastrous situation? Is it so awful, or were your fears exaggerated? Again, imagining that it has already happened: What are you going to do now? From this catastrophic situation what are your plans? How are you going

to cope with it? What could you have done to lessen its negative effects? (Imagine yourself saying 'things wouldn't be so bad if only I ...'.)

Step 3

When you have answered these questions, you will probably find that:

(a) Many possible catastrophes are not really as bad as your first, unconsidered, fears.
(b) You have identified some of the plans and actions that you can implement to lessen either the probability of the catastrophe's occurrence or the severity of its effects.
(c) You have prepared some contingency plans for coping with the catastrophe should it occur. These will be helpful in themselves and, by reducing the ambiguity and helplessness of the situation, you will have lessened your fear of it.

You should now be able to overcome the blockage and make your decisions.

Follow-up

When drawing up your contingency plans, Activities 16 (*Planning Change*) and 41 (*Action Planning*) will be helpful.

The study of disasters and especially so-called 'disaster planning' is a recent growth industry, much of which is a specialized field of work. There are a plethora of resources on the web including special sites for health, schools, churches and libraries. A simple two-page guide to contingency planning for small companies in particular can be found at: www.contingency-planning-disaster-recovery-guide.co.uk/.

At the corporate level, *Disaster Recovery Planning* by Jon Toigo (Prentice-Hall, 4th edition, 2013) is an expensive but comprehensive guide to all aspects of disaster recovery and business continuity planning, including risk management, information governance, security, availability and data management.

Critical Thinking

Managerial qualities	**Analytical skills:** Professional knowledge and skills: Emotional resilience: Mental agility

Critical thinking is an important aspect of managerial practice across all professional fields. As we become more saturated with information, misinformation and opinions, the ability to sort the wheat from the chaff and to discriminate between the vital and the trivial becomes ever more essential.

Critical thinking has been defined as *the art of analyzing and evaluating thinking with a view to improving it* (Paul and Elder, 2006, p. 4), so the aim is not just analysis, but action. Critical thinking is closely associated with *Reflective Practice* (see Activity 19) because it depends on the person first being able to reflect on their practice at the same time as being engaged in demanding professional work and complex technical tasks. In such situations, 'best practices' are not enough; changing circumstances and particular contexts require you to employ your critical thinking skills to continually reflect on what you are doing and how you could do it better.

There are several key things you can do with your ability to think critically. First and most obviously, it helps you to detect the underlying assumptions and perspectives that underlie what people say. Try the following activity:

Activity 1: Different Voices

Take a situation from your life where there is some controversy surrounding a particular course of action. This could be any situation where there is no

obvious right answer, perhaps an aspect of strategy for your organization – should we open up this new market, for example – or from where you live – should we ban cars from the High Street, for instance.

Step 1

Take six file cards and write on each a different standpoint from which critical voices of any course of action could come. For example:

Manager		Parent
Chief executive		Teacher
Main supplier	OR	Neighbour
Customer		Police officer
Local politician		Child
Environmental campaigner		Child psychologist

Step 2

When you have written these 'voices' on the cards, shuffle them and place them face down on the table. Now draw a card and think about the situation from that person's point of view – what would they say about the proposed course of action?

Make a brief note of what you think on the card under that person's name.

Shuffle the pack once more, choose another card and repeat. Give each voice the time and space in your mind to 'speak'.

Step 3

When you have written some notes for all the voices, take some time to read them all through. Ask yourself the following questions:

- ■ Are there any surprises for you?
- ■ Have you heard anything new?
- ■ How might seeing all these viewpoints influence what you would do next in this situation?

If you find it hard to find all the different voices on your own, an alternative is to try this out with family and friends or with a group of colleagues at work (as *Activity 2: Alternative Stances* below). Have them first brainstorm the key actors in the situation, write these down on separate cards, shuffle the cards and ask each person present to choose a card at random. Then have them speak from that 'voice' or standpoint, and finally discuss together the outcomes and the implications.

Discussion

Activity 1: Different Voices demonstrates how critical thinking involves not only reflecting on the assumptions underlying our own and other people's actions, but that it also means considering different ways of acting and living. So, this is not a passive, internal process but an active enquiry combining reflective analysis and informed action. It is an action learning process.

An action learning set is perhaps the ideal place to do this work. Here, as members get to know and to trust each other, the purpose is to support and challenge each person to learn and to act.

In considering the quandaries of action in situations where there are no simple answers, critical thinking leads into an analysis and understanding of vested interests and power dynamics. Any action in such conditions is likely to involve the mobilization and use of power in various relationships and often presents people with difficult ethical choices and dilemmas.

These are the tough and sticky situations in life where getting it wrong can have serious and long-term consequences. Critical thinking is the means for getting our heads straight and our vision clear, especially if we are lucky enough to have help from a few critical but supportive friends. However, the act of critical thinking can by itself get us into trouble. Challenging assumptions and exploring alternatives involves taking risks with other people because it involves questioning existing ways of doing things and criticizing established solutions. In some organizations, managerial work is still seen largely as technical problem-solving; instrumental work to do with making things work and not asking too many questions. In such conditions, becoming more critical may be misunderstood, seen as disloyal and may ultimately lead to the critic becoming marginalized and alienated from their local culture.

For this reason, peer groups such as action learning sets are a vital support for critical thinking efforts in many organizations and situations. Without this support and the protection of confidentiality, there is a danger that free and clear thinking is suppressed.

In Activity 1, people are developing their 'ordinary criticality' – an awareness of underlying assumptions and alternative perspectives – which does not necessarily reach the level of a social or organizational critique of power inequalities and the suppression of particular voices. *Activity 2: Alternative Stances* is designed to explore the political and ethical aspects of critical thinking, where the alternative voices come from different value positions likely to be fundamentally critical of any existing state of affairs.

Activity 2: Alternative Stances

You can attempt Activity 2 on your own, but it is usually better done in a group or team and is presented here from that perspective. This is an unusual group activity in that it works best in a virtual rather than a face-to-face setting. This is because the virtual setting provides each person with time to think and perhaps to read up on their stance.

Step 1

Choose a problem situation from your work, one that is shared and recognized by other people such as the members of your department or your professional network. Choose a difficult one; one that seems especially complex or confusing, perhaps a complicated or 'political' situation or one in which you are faced with a seemingly impossible dilemma.

Step 2

Recruit an e-mail group of colleagues or network members to work with you on this issue. Invite five or six people to join you in a discussion of a problem and warn them that you will be allocating a particular position to them from which you want them to argue and participate.

Step 3

When you have your e-mail group, write a statement briefly describing your issue or dilemma (100 or so words) ending with the question of what should be done.

At the foot of this description allocate one of the following stances to each person in the group (you can choose your own stances to suit of course, but make them politically diverse):

1. Marxist
2. Feminist
3. Environmentalist
4. Free market economist
5. NIMBY (Not In My Back Yard)
6. Anti-colonial campaigner

Ask each person to respond to the e-mail – *from their allocated stance* and in the voice they imagine such a position to use – within, say, 7 days. The aim is to work from that value position to propose an analysis and suggestions for action.
Stress that all exchanges will be kept confidential.

You can also suggest that people do any research they wish to work out their stance and the likely position to be taken on the issue.

Step 4

When all the stances have been posted, summarize the various analyses and proposals, together with any new thoughts, insights or questions that have come to you as a result of the exchanges.

Circulate your findings and perhaps, if you have new and pressing questions, ask for another round of contributions. Finally, invite members to comment on the findings and the process in which they have taken part.

Discussion

Activity 2: Alternative Stances involves you and others in taking some risks: raising the problem situation, choosing some people to work with – and for those people, saying what they think, albeit from an assumed position. However, the risks are mitigated by the controlled and confidential nature of the exchange, and this could be a useful way to rehearse possible options in a risky situation.

In many ways, the action learning set referred to earlier is the ideal group in which to try this activity, but of course not everyone is lucky enough to have such a set at hand. The e-mail group is an interesting method and should be easy enough to construct. If you choose people who are close by, then you can end this activity by suggesting a face-to-face meeting over coffee or lunch to digest the outcomes and to help you identify your next steps with the issue.

Follow-up

Critical thinking is perhaps the most-cited meta-goal in secondary and higher education and there is a great deal of material available, especially for educators. There is a well-established journal, *Inquiry: Critical Thinking across the Disciplines,* dedicated to the topic and its applications in many professionals fields, while Critical Thinking On The Web (austhink.com/critical/) is a website of websites and a useful place to start.

There are also many books on the theme. Dorothy Strachan's *Making Questions Work: A Guide to What and How to Ask for Facilitators, Consultants, Managers, Coaches and Educators* (Jossey-Bass, 2007) is a useful resource with a section on critical thinking. *Critical Thinking: An Exploration of Theory and Practice* by Jennifer Moon (Taylor & Francis, 2012) is another down-to-earth guide aimed at educators and teachers in schools and higher education.

Reflective Practice

Managerial qualities	**Analytical skills:** Professional knowledge and skills: Emotional resilience: Mental agility

Reflective practice is closely associated with *Critical Thinking* (see Activity 18). It is hard to think critically if you haven't first developed the habit and skills of reflection.

What do we mean by reflection? In the novels of Henry James, 'not much happens' because much of the text is devoted to the inner thoughts of the main characters. This is the classical meaning of reflection, where thought is for the sake of itself and not necessarily for action. By contrast, Donald Schön's 'Reflective Practitioner' (1991) aims at effective action, and is someone who is able to reflect on what they are doing at the same time as they are doing it. Schön was critical of managers and professionals who rely on 'technical rationality' and rule-following. These 'expert professionals' are frequently found to be wrong and misleading in complex and changing circumstances. Today, we recognize that every professional manager must not only be able to handle the complex technical requirements of their work, but also to have the ability to reflect on their practice and to adapt and flex their actions as necessary.

The effective manager is able to 'read' work situations: sensing what is happening, being aware of the elements and factors involved, and of the way in which these factors are related. When successful, we can recognize the effects of these factors on our own actions and, conversely, the effects of our behaviour on these factors. We are able to use this awareness and sensitivity to learn from everyday experiences.

A model of thinking, feeling and acting

A good way of developing the habit of reflective practice is to keep a *Personal Journal* (Activity 8). The model from that activity is used here to make a more detailed analysis of your behaviour and actions in a particular situation.

1. *THOUGHTS AND IDEAS*: in any situation we have a number of thoughts and ideas about what is going on and what we might do about it. These thoughts will depend on the various elements present and on our own assumptions and the perceptions brought in from previous experiences. Also important are any new ideas triggered by the new situation.
2. *FEELINGS*: the way we act is partly determined by our feelings in a given situation. We are often unaware or only partly aware of our feelings and the effect they are having on our behaviour. There is often a learned tendency to suppress or deny feelings and to keep 'a stiff upper lip' – but if you are to be in control of your actions, it is essential to be sensitive to your feelings and their effects.
3. *ACTION-TENDENCIES*: we also have various action-tendencies, which are internal motivations or predispositions that push individuals towards certain types of action or inaction. For example, although disagreeing strongly with someone in a meeting, I might not say anything because I don't like challenging authority. This fear or lack of confidence leads to an action-tendency of saying/doing nothing. Another action-tendency could be a strong need to *do* something, to be impulsive rather than think things through carefully.

Each of these three elements influences our actions and behaviour. In the example of the meeting above: my *thoughts/ideas* are that what has been said is wrong and my *feelings* are those of concern or excitement. However, due to my other feeling of fear of challenging authority, my *action-tendency* is to say nothing.

How I act in this situation depends on which of the three wins out. Will my ideas and half my feelings overcome my action-tendency, leading to a soundly presented contribution? Or will my other feelings combine with my negative action-tendencies, leading me to remain silent? Or will my feelings and action-tendencies result in my making a fumbling, incoherent statement that prevents my beautifully logical ideas from getting a fair hearing?

The three elements depend on each other. For example, my thoughts and ideas about what is being said partly depend upon my feelings about the person saying it – and vice versa. So although this model of behaviour is simple enough, it represents a very complicated situation. Figure A19.1 shows the links between these thoughts/ideas, feelings and action-tendencies.

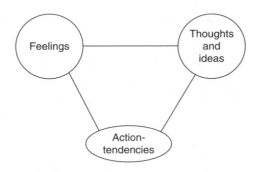

Figure A19.1   Links between thoughts/ideas, feelings and action-tendencies

In practice, of course, any situation occurs as a sequence of events. Our thoughts/ideas, feelings and action-tendencies arise in response to situations, themselves affected by previous events, and our subsequent actions then lead to new situations and so on (Figure A19.2).

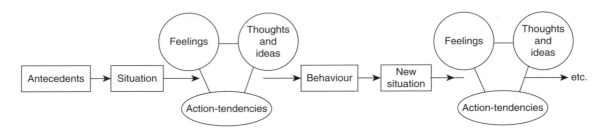

Figure A19.2   The effect situational stimuli have on thoughts/ideas, feelings and action-tendencies

Activity

This activity is in two steps. The first looks at some past events and asks you to reflect on them. The second step invites you to reflect on current situations.

Step 1

Choose a recent significant event that was challenging or difficult. Who else was involved in this situation? Choose the two or three most significant actors alongside yourself.

Now reflect back on the circumstances leading up to the event. Cast your mind back and recall your own feelings, thought/ideas, action-tendencies and

behaviour in the situation. Note these down using the first column in Table A19.1.

Table A19.1   Events and responses

What happened	My responses
_____	My feelings
_____	
_____	_____
	_____
_____	My thoughts and ideas
_____	
_____	_____
	_____
_____	My action-tendencies
_____	
_____	_____
	_____
_____	Hence . . . My behaviour
_____	
_____	_____
_____	_____

Now try to identify these elements for each of the main people involved. This will be difficult because we don't really *know* how someone else is feeling, but have a go at guessing or estimating – which is what we normally do. If you have difficulty doing this, the best source of information is always the people themselves. If this is possible, why not check it out with them?

Before moving on, think about the significance of the feelings that you were unable to identify, or that you assumed incorrectly:

■   Are you better at estimating feelings, ideas or action-tendencies?

_____

_____

■ Are there some people whose reactions you can perceive accurately, and others you cannot?

_____

_____

Once you have reflected on this, fill out the second column in Table A19.1. What were your perceptions of your own and others' responses *during* the event? Again, check with the others if necessary. Finally, add the responses *after* the event.

Study your table and reflect on:

■ In what ways were the responses related to each other? What caused what?

_____

_____

■ How do you feel about the way you handled the situation? What, if anything, could you have done differently? What do you think the consequences would have been?

_____

_____

■ What can you learn from this?

_____

_____

Step 2

Once you have practised reflecting on a past event, now apply it to a current situation – something of significance with which you are now involved. Using Table A19.1 again:

1. Reflect on the situation so far and fill in as many of the responses as you can for yourself and the other main actors. If you are able, check your perceptions of their responses.
2. How do you feel about the way the situation is shaping up so far? What are you going to do? What do you think the consequences will be?

3. Do what you have decided to do.
4. Continue with your reflections. Are the effects as predicted?

Repeat steps (1–4) until you think the event is over.

What have you learned from this event? What are the implications of this learning for your future actions?

The ability to reflect in the midst of situations like this is an important quality and should become part of your everyday managerial life. Start considering important or significant situations in terms of the perceptions and responses of the other people involved, and then checking these out to make sure that you are not basing your actions on invalid assumptions.

Follow-up

Reflective practice has become an accepted part of effective working in complex or contested situations. As well as a good explanation on Wikipedia, there is a five-minute video on YouTube that provides an introduction to reflective practice at work: www.youtube.com/watch?v = 1AfHPV-YBdI.

The Open University has a comprehensive paper that covers the origins, models and critiques of the idea of reflective practice at: www.open.ac.uk/cetl-workspace/cetlcontent/.../4bf2b48887459.pdf.

There are also many books and an academic journal on the theme. Donald Schön's classic text *The Reflective Practitioner: How Professionals Think in Action* (Basic Books, 1991) is still well worth reading for its lucid text and fundamental insight, which is as valid as it ever was. *Reflective Practice in the Lifelong Learning Sector* by Judi Roffey-Barentsen and Richard Malthouse (Learning Matters, 2009) is a book aimed at trainers and teachers, and at people concerned with Continuing Professional Development (CPD). It is very easy to use and gives clear explanations on how to get the most from reflective practice.

Asserting Yourself

Managerial qualities	**Analytical skills:** People skills: Emotional resilience: Initiative

Assertiveness is a key skill for managers and leaders. Some of us are naturally assertive; others have to work at it. It is easy to confuse assertiveness with 'pushiness' or aggression. In fact, assertiveness means pursuing your goals *and* the goals of the other people in the situation. It means getting a positive result in unclear or difficult situations where the temptation is to hold back or let things go.

Activity

Step 1

In the following questionnaire, you will find 10 sets of three statements, similar to the following example:

I'm a person who:

(a) has my rights violated
(b) protects my own rights
(c) violates the rights of others

The scoring is based on the notion that we all behave in each of these ways from time to time, although the extent to which we have a tendency for (a), (b) or (c) will vary.

You are therefore asked to allocate points to each of (a), (b) and (c), such that the total adds up to 10. Thus, if you think that you quite often have your rights violated, and quite often protect the rights of others, but rarely violate the rights of others, you might score yourself as a person who:

(a) has my rights violated | 4
(b) protects my own rights | 4
(c) violates the rights of others | 2
| **10**

On the other hand, if you recognize that you protect your own rights at all costs, even if this quite often involves violating the rights of others, then your scores might be as follows:

(a) has my rights violated | 0
(b) protects my own rights | 6
(c) violates the rights of others. | 4
| **10**

Now complete the questionnaire.
I'm a person who:

1. (a) has my rights violated
   (b) protects my own rights
   (c) violates the rights of others
   | **10**

2. (a) does not achieve my goals
   (b) achieves my goals without hurting other people
   (c) achieves my goals at the expense of other people
   | **10**

3. (a) feels frustrated and unhappy
   (b) feels good about myself
   (c) is defensive and/or belligerent
   | **10**

4. (a) is inhibited and withdrawn
   (b) is socially and emotionally expressive
   (c) is explosive, hostile, angry
   | **10**

5. (a) feels hurt, anxious
    (b) is quietly self-confident
    (c) is brashly confident, boastful

    [ ]
    [ ]
    [ ]
    [10]

6. (a) fails to achieve my goals
    (b) tries to find ways so that I can achieve my goals *and*
         others can achieve theirs
    (c) is not concerned about others and their goals

    [ ]
    [ ]
    [ ]
    [10]

7. (a) is gullible, easily taken in
    (b) is open-minded and questioning
    (c) is suspicious, cynical

    [ ]
    [ ]
    [ ]
    [10]

8. (a) feels bad about my weaknesses
    (b) is aware of my weaknesses, but don't dislike myself because
         of them
    (c) is unaware of my weaknesses

    [ ]
    [ ]
    [ ]
    [10]

9. (a) allows others to choose for me
    (b) chooses for myself
    (c) intrudes on other people's choices

    [ ]
    [ ]
    [ ]
    [10]

10. (a) is taken advantage of
    (b) protects my own rights
    (c) takes advantage of others

    [ ]
    [ ]
    [ ]
    [10]

Step 2

This questionnaire is based on a model that suggests that ASSERTION is the 'happy medium' between two equally undesirable extremes – *passivity* and *aggression*.

To see where you are, add up all your (a) scores (*passivity*), (b) scores (*assertion*) and (c) scores (*aggression*) and enter them in Figure A20.1.

This way of looking at assertion is very important. Although it is easy to distinguish assertion from passivity, it is often mistaken and confused with aggression. In fact, as the questionnaire statements show, they are very different.

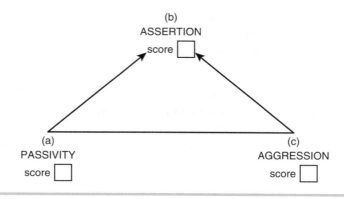

Figure A20.1   Scoring model

Step 3

Construct an action plan to build up your assertiveness. You can use Activity 41, *Action Planning*, for this. The (b) behaviours tell you what to aim for if you want to become more assertive; these can become the basis of your intentions for actions.

Learning to be assertive takes practice. You have taken the important first step by getting an idea of your passive/assertive/aggressive profile.

Another useful step is to ask other people to fill the questionnaire out on you – what is *their* picture of where you are?

Then ask them: 'In order to become more assertive, what should I . . .

1. . . . do less of?'
2. . . . do more of?'
3. . . . start doing?'

Another tip is to keep a diary of how assertive you are at work and outside. You can use Activity 8, *Personal Journal*, for this. Record your experiences for 2–3 weeks, trying to log at least one situation per day. When you have a set of data – analyse it: Do certain situations or people tend to push you into passivity or aggression? What is there about these? What can you do about them?

Other Activities in this book that will help you with ideas about how to build your assertiveness include those concerned with power, such as Activities 9 (*Use Your Power*), 11 (*Political Awareness*), 43 (*Managing Upwards*) and 52 (*Managing Your Dependency*).

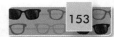

Follow-up

There are lots of books on assertiveness. Alec Grimsley's *Vital Conversations: A Practical Approach to Handling Difficult Conversations, Managing Conflict, Giving Feedback and Influencing Difficult People* (Barnes Holland, 2010) is widely praised, while *Assertiveness at Work: A Practical Guide to Handling Awkward Situations* by Ken Back and Kate Back (McGraw-Hill, 3rd edition, 2005) has stood the test of time.

A web search on assertiveness training produces over 2 million entries. Take your pick!

Handling Conflicts

Managerial qualities	**People skills:** Emotional resilience: Sensitivity to events

Handling conflict is an important part of leadership and managerial work. You may need to mediate between conflicting people or be in conflict yourself with someone else competing for the same resources as you. You will certainly be handling crises and unforeseen events.

Conflict situations occur when one party frustrates the goals of other parties and yet they are dependent on each other. The outcomes can vary from an outright battle through negotiations and compromise, to walkovers or avoidance. In particular situations, one response might be more appropriate than another, but no one response is correct every time.

Think about how you respond to conflict. How do you react when faced with frustration and antagonism? The more aware you are of your own personal style, and the larger your repertoire of responses, the more flexible and successful you will be in resolving particular conflicts.

This activity will help you to look at your usual responses to conflict situations and generate some alternatives for action. It is in three parts: Part 1 contains three case studies to test your responses to particular conflict situations; Part 2 offers a model of conflict resolution styles; and Part 3 is a questionnaire to help you determine your preferred approach.

Activity

Part 1: Case studies

For each of the three short case studies, write down your first reaction to the situation. Think yourself into the situation and feel the anger, frustration or whatever wells up inside you.

Case 1

You have just arrived at the coffee room and are waiting for your coffee. Across the room you see a colleague with whom you fell out at the last department meeting. The argument concerned the shortage of skilled staff – you believe your department does not get its fair share but that your colleague's is overstaffed. This morning one of your staff failed to report for work and on applying for a pool consultant you were told that the last one had gone to your colleague's department. At the sight of this person, your anger and sense of injustice flood back. What do you do? (Write down your first reaction.)

_____

_____

_____

_____

_____

Case 2

The road on which you live on has a fringe of lawn between the footpath and the road. You look after your section and like to see it looking green and well tended. Most of your neighbours do the same, but on one side of you live some people you don't know too well and who ignore this common policy. They never look after the verge and they and their friends frequently park their cars on it. Recently, they have been parking on your section and, in the recent wet weather, tyre marks have marred the green surface. You have spoken to them once about this, but they appeared off-hand and indifferent to your concern. One Sunday morning you wake at 5 a.m. to an engine noise, and on looking outside see two deep scars across your lawn. At 9 a.m. and still annoyed, you meet your neighbour in the newsagents. What do you do? (Write down your first reaction.)

_____

_____

_____

_____

_____

Case 3

You are a young manager in the sales section of a large company. Your boss sends for you one morning and you hear on the grapevine that you will be asked to take on an unpopular duty that involves coming in every other Saturday. You don't like it – you like to keep your weekends free for the family, and you feel you are getting a raw deal because you are junior. You're on your way to the boss's office. What do you do? (Write down your first reaction.)

_____

_____

_____

_____

_____

When you have responded to these three cases, go back over them and see if you can think of *alternative* approaches.

Case 1: Alternative approaches

_____

_____

_____

_____

_____

Case 2: Alternative approaches

_____

_____

_____

_____

_____

Case 3: Alternative approaches

_____

_____

_____

_____

_____

One effect of conflict is that it can lead to stress, rigidity and a hardening of attitudes, which partly explains why we have habitual ways of reacting to conflict situations. Address the following questions:

■ Looking back over your initial reactions to the three cases, can you spot a habitual mode of response?

_____

_____

■ Think of conflicts you have had in the past with your spouse, colleagues, parents, etc. Do these show any pattern of response?

_____

_____

■ Of the three cases, how many alternatives to each of your initial responses could you generate? Two? Three? Four? Or more?

_____

_____

The more alternatives you generate, the more chances you have of being flexible in practice.

Part 2: A conflict resolution model

Figure A21.1 shows five conflict-handling styles based on two basic dimensions of conflict situations – in any conflict between two parties the mode of resolution depends upon:

(a) how assertive or unassertive each party is in pursuing its *own goals*
(b) how cooperative or uncooperative each party is in pursuing *the goals of the other*.

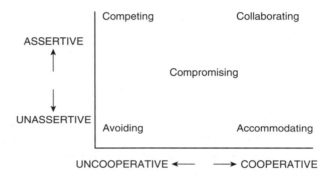

Figure A21.1 Conflict style model

Because conflict resolution is an interactive and reciprocal activity, the style you adopt will affect the style of your partner, and vice versa. If both of you are highly assertive yet uncooperative in terms of each other's goals, then they will adopt a battling, *competing* style; if you are both unassertive of your own goals and also uncooperative, you will tend to avoid the conflict altogether and try to pretend it doesn't exist. And so on.

Use the model in Figure A21.1 to diagnose a conflict situation in which you have been personally involved (a personal relationship perhaps offers most scope). Can you classify the modes adopted by the two parties and arrive at a description of the joint style of resolution on the chart?

Do this with as many conflict situations as you can think of. By diagnosing your habitual responses in certain situations and observing the responses of others, you can obtain a clearer picture of your own behaviour. Answer the following questions:

■ When do you avoid conflict?

_____

_____

■ When do you compete with others?

_____

_____

■ Do you ever collaborate in conflict situations?

_____

_____

■ How do you feel when you accommodate others?

_____

_____

■ How often do you secure compromises?

_____

_____

The more you can identify your own style(s) and the responses generated by others, and the more alternatives you can see in any particular situation, the more likely you are to behave appropriately the next time conflict arises.

Part 3: Conflict management questionnaire

This Paired-comparison Questionnaire will help you to identify your preferred style of conflict handling.

Choose one of the statements from each of the 30 pairs below. _Choose the one which is most like the way you handle differences between yourself and others:_

1. 1. I am usually firm in pursuing my goals.
   2. I attempt to get all concerns and issues immediately out in the open.
2. 1. I put my cards on the table and invite the other person to do likewise.
   2. When conflicts arise, I try to win my case.
3. 1. Once I adopt a position I defend it strongly.

    2. I prefer not to argue but to look for the best solution possible.

4. 1. I sometimes sacrifice my own wishes for the wishes of the other person.
    2. I feel that differences are not always worth worrying about.

5. 1. I accept the views of the other, rather than rock the boat.
    2. I avoid people with strong views.

6. 1. I like to cooperate with others and follow their ideas.
    2. I feel that most things are not worth arguing about. I stick to my own views.

7. 1. I try to find some compromise situation.
    2. I am usually firm in pursuing my goals.

8. 1. When conflicts arise, I try to win my case.
    2. I propose a middle ground.

9. 1. I like to meet the other person half-way.
    2. Once I adopt a position I defend it strongly.

10. 1. I feel that differences are not always worth worrying about.
    2. I try to find a compromise solution.

11. 1. I propose a middle ground.
    2. I avoid people with strong views.

12. 1. I feel that most things are not worth arguing about. I stick to my own views.
    2. I like to meet the other person half-way.

13. 1. I am usually firm in pursuing my goals.
    2. I sometimes sacrifice my own wishes for the wishes of the other person.

14. 1. I accept the views of the other, rather than rock the boat.
    2. When conflicts arise, I try to win my case.

15. 1. Once I adopt a position I defend it strongly.
    2. I like to cooperate with others and follow their ideas.

16. 1. I try to find a compromise solution.
    2. I sometimes sacrifice my own wishes for the wishes of the other person.

17. 1. I accept the views of the other, rather than rock the boat.
    2. I propose a middle ground.

18. 1. I like to meet the other person half-way.
    2. I like to cooperate with others and follow their ideas.

19. 1. I feel that differences are not always worth worrying about.
    2. I am usually firm in pursuing my goals.

20. 1. When conflicts arise, I try to win my case.
    2. I avoid people with strong views.

21. 1. I feel that most things are not worth arguing about. I stick to my own views.
    2. Once I adopt a position I defend it strongly.

22. 1. I attempt to get all concerns and issues immediately out in the open.

2. I feel that differences are not always worth worrying about.

23. 1. I avoid people with strong views.

    2. I put my cards on the table and invite the other person to do likewise.

24. 1. I prefer not to argue but to look for the best solution possible.

    2. I feel that most things are not worth arguing about. I stick to my own views.

25. 1. I attempt to get all concerns and issues immediately out in the open.

    2. I try to find a compromise solution.

26. 1. I put my cards on the table and invite the other person to do likewise.

    2. I propose a middle ground.

27. 1. I prefer not to argue but to look for the best solution possible.

    2. I like to meet the other person half-way.

28. 1. I sometimes sacrifice my own wishes for the wishes of the other person.

    2. I attempt to get all concerns and issues immediately out in the open.

29. 1. I put my cards on the table and invite the other person to do likewise.

    2. I accept the views of the other, rather than rock the boat.

30. 1. I like to cooperate with others and follow their ideas.

    2. I prefer not to argue but to look for the best solution possible.

Scoring

The key below shows you how to score your questionnaire (Table A21.1).

A, B, C, D and E represent the five conflict-handling styles as follows:

A = Avoiding
B = Accommodating
C = Compromising
D = Competing
E = Collaborating.

So, for example, if you chose the second statement of the first pair, then you would score 1 for E. If you chose the first statement of the second pair, you would score another 1 for E, and so on (see Table A21.1).

The maximum score for any mode is 12 and the total aggregate score is 30. *A score of more than 6 on any mode would indicate a preference for that mode, while a score of less than 6 would indicate relative neglect.*

What do these results mean to you?

■ Do you have some dominant ways of approaching conflicts?
■ Are there styles that you do not make use of?
■ What would you like to change?

Table A21.1   Conflict management questionnaire

Statement pair	Conflict resolution mode				
	A	B	C	D	E
1				1	2
2				2	1
3				1	2
4	2	1			
5	2	1			
6	2	1			
7			1	2	
8			2	1	
9			1	2	
10	1		2		
11	2		1		
12	1		2		
13		2		1	
14		1		2	
15		2		1	
16		2	1		
17		1	2		
18		2	1		
19	1			2	
20	2			1	
21	1			2	
22	2				1
23	1				2
24	2				1
25			2		1
26			2		1
27			2		1
28		1			2
29		2			1
30		1			2
Total					

The questionnaire is a one-point-in-time measure of your reaction to conflict situations. It has validity in so far it corroborates with your own perception of your preferred style and the results you got from the cases earlier in this exercise. If these point in the same direction, then a conclusion is comparatively simple. More uneven results will require puzzling out. Other people's opinions will be especially useful here – particularly those with whom you have had your differences!

You need practice to develop skills in resolving conflicts. Activity 20, *Asserting Yourself*, is relevant here because the ideas have a direct bearing on how you approach conflict situations. Activity 8, *Personal Journal*, could also be used to help you learn from your own conflict experiences.

Follow-up

Conflict is another popular topic on the web with millions of references. Like MindTools, which has material on both conflict and negotiation, BusinessBalls is a useful site with many simply explained tools and guides including negotiation: http://www.businessballs.com/negotiation.htm.

The best and most straightforward book on negotiating and conflict management is Roger Fisher and William Ury's *Getting to Yes: Negotiating an Agreement without Giving In* (Random House, 3rd edition, 2012). Every manager should have this book on their shelves.

Getting the Best Out of Groups

Managerial qualities	**People skills:** Sensitivity to events: Analysing skills: Initiative

How much of your time at work is spent in groups? Partnerships, project teams, committees, consortia and other meetings may account for over half of your time at work. The trend towards partnerships and shared leadership adds to this load.

Groups are used for many vital functions, especially in information sharing and making sense, reaching consensus and making decisions. All of these processes can be difficult and energy-consuming. Every leader and manager needs to learn about how to get the best out of groups and how to make teams as effective as possible.

The aim of this activity is to improve your understanding and skill in handling behaviour in groups. It does this by offering a process for observing behaviours in groups and also by inviting you to experiment with your own group behaviours.

Activity

Part 1: Measuring the contribution rate

A first exercise in group observation and analysis is to take a 'contribution count'. At your next meeting, choose a 10- or 15-minute period when you can concentrate on observing rather than contributing.

Write the name or identifying mark for each member of the group on a sheet of paper. Over 10 or 15 minutes, note each contribution made by each group member by putting a mark beside their names. See Figure A22.1, where the 'five-barred gate method' is used.

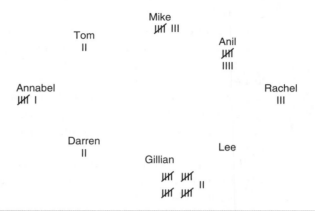

Figure A22.1   Contribution roles in a group

A 'contribution' is any spoken comment to the group (not an aside to another member), although it may be directed at one person in particular. It may be short or long, although you could put two marks for a contribution of more than, say, 30 seconds.

Figure A22.1 shows clear differences between the group members in terms of the number of contributions made:

Gillian 22 ⎱
Anil 9   ⎰ HIGH contributors

Mike 8   ⎱
Annabel 6   ⎰ MEDIUM contributors

Rachel 3   ⎫
Tom 2   ⎪
Darren 2   ⎬ LOW contributors
Lee 0   ⎭

Now, why did Gillian and Anil contribute most – because they have the most to say, or because they are the more senior? Either way, does their dominance help or hinder the group in its task? If they knew most about the subject under discussion, or because they were the two principal speakers for and against an idea, then this might well help the group achieve its goals.

What about Rachel, Tom, Darren and Lee? Did they just have nothing to contribute, or were they shut out, asleep, junior or 'unlistened-to' members?

Share your contribution count with the other members of your group – although you will need a good relationship or, better still, a contract with them to do this. If the group takes notice of the observation, it can provoke useful changes.

A contribution count can tell you a lot about a group, especially over a number of meetings. Behaviour patterns form quickly and we tend to conform to these – although this is done at a subconscious level of which we are not fully aware unless it is brought to our attention. Equally, a contribution count measures only a fraction of what goes on in a group situation, and it should not be taken for more than it is. It takes no account of the *quality* of the contribution, of non-verbal behaviour, of the requirements of the particular situation or of how people are feeling.

However, it has the great advantage of being easy to do. For a more advanced version of 'the contribution count', in your next meeting observe as before but now log in addition:

■ Who talks to whom. Who do they direct their remarks at and look at when they speak?
■ Who interrupts whom?
■ Who finally makes the decision – one person, two persons, the whole group?

These are more difficult to measure, but will give you useful data for your own reflection and, if you can introduce it, for the greater effectiveness of the group.

Part 2: Categorizing behaviour in groups

The effectiveness of groups depends largely upon right behaviour at the right time. The group behaviour categories shown in Table A22.1 were developed and pioneered by Neil Rackham and have been used to improve group effectiveness at British Airways and many other organizations.

There are nine categories for you to practise with. Again, chose a 10- to 15-minute session to observe. Use an observation sheet with categories down the left-hand side and group members' names along the top as in Table A22.2.

Practise on two or four behaviours and two or four people until you get the hang of it. Try logging Gillian and Anil on 'proposing', 'giving information', 'seeking information' and 'supporting/building'. High contributors often do a lot of proposing and giving information but less information seeking.

Some groups do a lot of giving information and making proposals, but do very little seeking information or understanding. Building and summarizing

Table A22.1 Categories of group behaviour

Category	Definition
Proposing	A behaviour which puts forward a new concept, suggestion or course of action: 'I suggest we call a meeting of all Department employees'
Giving information	A behaviour which offers facts, opinions or clarification to others: 'There is a full definition of this in the handbook'
Seeking information	A behaviour which seeks facts, opinions or clarification from others: 'What do the rest of you think?'
Supporting/building	A behaviour which declares support or agreement with another person or attempts to extend or develop a proposal made by another person: 'I agree with Lee and moreover we should start now'
Disagreeing	A behaviour which involves a direct criticism, difference of opinion or disagreement with another person's idea: 'No, my boss would never accept a reduction in his budget'
Defending/attacking	A behaviour which attacks another person or defends an individual's own position. More emotional than disagreeing: 'That is a stupid idea' or 'My idea is better than that'
Blocking/difficulty stating	A behaviour which blocks another proposal without offering alternatives and without reasons: 'It won't work' or 'We can't have that'
Testing understanding	A behaviour which checks and seeks to establish whether an earlier contribution has been understood: 'Can I just ask you, Anil, did you imply that you were supporting or not supporting Mike's proposal?'
Summarizing	A behaviour which summarizes, or restates concisely, the contest of a previous proposal or discussion: 'Well, so far, ladies and gentleman, we have heard two proposals: Tom's – to call a meeting immediately; and Anil's – to delay action until next week'

Table A22.2 Observation sheet for of group behaviour

Observation sheet	Date				Time				
Names	Anil	Gillian	Mike	Tom	Annabel	Lee	Rachel	Darren	Total
Proposing	II				I		I	I	16
Giving information	I	IIII		I	II	II	I	I	20
Seeking information	III	I		III					
and so on ...									

tend to be rare behaviours. 'Defending/attacking' creates similar responses in others, and a sort of escalation or spiral occurs.

From your observations over a number of meetings and 15-minute periods you should be able to answer some of the following:

- Do people fall into habitual roles? Are there habitual low contributors or chronic proposers or consenters who do no disagreeing?
- Is there a balance of behaviour in the group? People may fall into particular roles, but if these complement each other then the group may function well. But unless somebody *is* doing the summarizing, testing understanding, supporting, etc., several vital functions will be missing.
- How could this group work better? For example, does everybody feel okay about their roles, levels of contribution and rewards from this group? Does the group make good decisions without undue wasting of time?

Good groups will welcome your observations, but many groups are unused to self-scrutiny and may be defensive. Caution is recommended.

Part 3

You can dispense with the caution and be as experimental as you like with your own behaviour. After your observations you will have some ideas about the way you behave in groups. Spend some time now summarizing these.

Step 1

What characteristics have you noticed in yourself?

- Are you a medium, low or high contributor?
- Are you a proposer, a builder or what?
- How much seeking behaviour do you practise?
- What happened the last time you were in a defending/attacking position?
- How often do you test your understanding of other people's ideas?

Step 2

Now do some experimenting. Choose some of the behaviours that you would like to do more of, and some you'd like to cut back on and follow the steps below:

2.1. At the next meeting you attend, experiment by using one new behaviour. If you're trying to lessen a behaviour, try cutting it out altogether. What is this behaviour?

2.2. Carefully observe what effect you're having. You may be able to obtain feedback on how people react to you in the meeting or through conversations afterwards.

2.3. If you're stuck for behaviours to try, remember that seeking information, building, summarizing and testing understanding are often low in groups.

Here are some suggested actions. At the next meeting try one of the following:

- Do nothing but ask questions.
- Never ask a question.
- Do not agree or disagree with anything.
- Each time you're not absolutely sure what another person means, ask for clarification.
- If you're normally a high contributor – say nothing; if you're normally low – aim to say more than anyone else.

Follow-up

This type of analysis was first undertaken by Robert Bales and his colleagues more than 50 years ago. If you are interested in the study of groups, then David Buchanan and Andrej Huczynski's massive *Organisational Behaviour: An Introductory Text* (Financial Times/Prentice-Hall, 7th edition, 2010) devotes a major part to behaviour in groups.

If you are more concerned with the practical aspects of getting the best out of groups, then Jenny Rogers' *Facilitating Groups* (Open University/McGraw-Hill, 2010) is a readable guide that will help you in this task.

What Are You Like?

Managerial qualities	**People skills:** Self-knowledge: Analytical skills

Your success and failure in achieving things with and through people depend a lot on how you see and make judgements about other people and how you see yourself in relation to them.

Any action you take to influence another person is based on a complex set of assumptions about how they will interpret your action and the way in which they will respond to it.

Part 1 of this activity is designed to help you become aware of the ways in which you see other people and yourself. Part 2 suggests that you check this out to see how your perceptions coincide with those of others.

Activity

Part 1

Step 1

In Column 1 of Figure A23.1, write the names of five people with whom you interact frequently at work.

Columns 2 and 3 of Figure A23.1 each have ten boxes, joined in pairs by horizontal lines. The lines represent dimensions of difference between people.

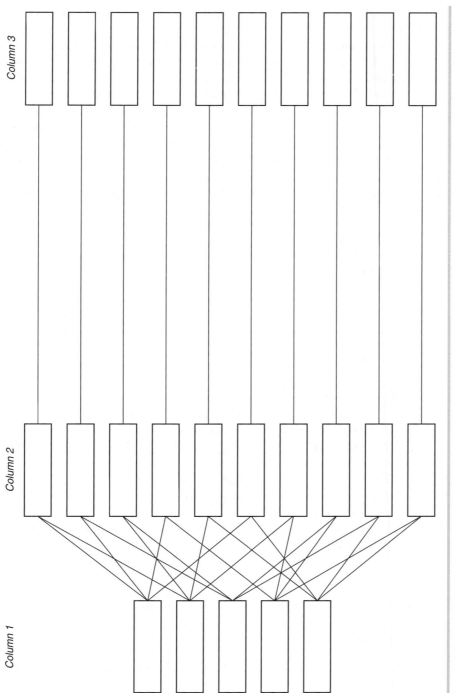

Figure A23.1

For example: kind–aloof; aggressive–meek, clever–stupid; honest–devious, and so on.

Take each dimension in turn and look at the names of the people in the two boxes joined to it by the lines between Columns 1 and 2. Think of a way in which these two people seem different to you in some way, and a pair of words such as the ones given above which describes the difference you perceive between them.

Put one word in the box at each end of the dimension (it doesn't matter which word goes at which end). Do this for each of the ten dimensions, using a different dimension (and therefore pair of words) each time. As this is a short activity, don't worry that you haven't covered all the differences between people; the idea is to get a sense of the ways in which you classify people.

Step 2

Now, treating each of the ten dimensions as a scale, put a cross to show where you think you are as a person, and mark it with your initials (see Figure A23.2).

Figure A23.2

Think of each scale as running from extreme to extreme, e.g. 'very reliable' to 'very unreliable', even if the people from whom you derived this dimension in the first place are not at the extremes.

Now think about yourself and your close working colleagues. How do you see yourself in relation to them?

The dimensions that you have chosen are ways in which you distinguish between people – therefore, they are likely to be important qualities or characteristics in your eyes.

Does this give you a sense of how you make judgements about people and on what grounds?

Part 2

If Part 1 gave you useful food for thought about yourself in relation to your colleagues, you can take this activity further with some of the following possibilities:

(a) Decide what you would want to be like by ticking the dimensions where you would like to be.
(b) Try *being* different. If you can do so, is it what you really want?

(c) Choose one of your five colleagues; mark where you think they are on each dimension and then show it to him or her. How do they see themselves compared with your view?

(d) Repeat (c) with other colleagues.

The key to understanding how you see yourself and others is to develop the habit of checking your perceptions with the people with whom you work.

Follow-up

This activity is based on George Kelly's Personal Construct Psychology (PCP) and his Repertory Grid methodology. There are many explanations of this on the web, together with software tools to apply Rep Grids. If you want to start with an explanation, see: en.wikipedia.org/wiki/Repertory_grid

Also see Activity 12, *Credulous Listening*, for some follow-up references on PCP.

Getting to Know You

Managerial qualities	**People skills:** Self-knowledge

To know someone well, we need to get beyond the trivial. Getting to know someone involves learning more about them, their ideas, hopes, fears and ambitions. For the other person to reveal these things about themselves, it is likely that we will have to reveal significant aspects of ourselves and of our lives in turn. This mutual exchange of personal information can lead to a better understanding and acceptance of each other.

However, our natural reticence and everyday social norms usually stop us talking so openly even with fairly close acquaintances. This activity can be used in any situation where you want to get to know somebody reasonably well, reasonably quickly. At the same time, you'll find that sharing this personal information will increase your own self-understanding.

Activity

Before you undertake this activity with anyone, make sure that each of you *wants* to get to know the other better. You can't do this unless you are both 'up for it'.

Find a place where you won't be disturbed and set aside at least an hour.

Instructions

Read the following instructions carefully before looking at Table A24.1.

Table A24.1 consists of a set of incomplete statements. Start with the first one, and take it in turn to complete the statements, telling the other person as much or as little as you want. *N.B. It is entirely up to each person to decide how much or how little to say.* Your partner can respond to what you say in any way they like. Then the other person completes the statement as above. When you have both said enough, move on to Statement 2, and so on.

Table A24.1   **The statements**

1. My name is ...
2. My job is ...
3. My age is ...
4. I live ...
5. I was born in ...
6. My previous jobs included ...
7. Things I like best about this job are ...
8. Things I like least about this job are ...
9. To me, being a woman/man ...
10. My marital status is ...
11. Children ...
12. My parents ...
13. My friends ...
14. My hobbies/spare-time activities ...
15. When I get to work ...
16. When I leave work ...
17. At this very minute, I feel ...
18. Ideally, this time next year ...
19. In the long term, my ambition is ...
20. The trouble with this organization is ...
21. My idea of an ideal holiday would be ...
22. Things that I find very difficult ...
23. If the worst comes to the worst in 12 months' time ...
24. The sort of things I worry about ...
25. What this country needs ...
26. My religious beliefs ...
27. To me, being black/white ...
28. My secret fears ...
29. My feelings about you are ...
30. My feelings about myself are ...

Don't look ahead at the other statements – concentrate only on the one being discussed.

Stop this activity whenever either of you wishes to do so.

Follow-up

Having finished this activity:

■ What did you learn about yourself and the other person?

_____

_____

_____

_____

_____

■ Do you think that it has improved your relationship?

_____

_____

_____

_____

_____

Getting to Yes

Managerial qualities	**People skills:** Emotional resilience: Sensitivity to events

Getting to Yes *[by Fisher and Ury] is by far the best thing I've ever read about negotiation.*

J.K. Galbraith

Step 1

Consider the following statements and decide which list – A or B – best describes how you are likely to behave in a negotiation:

A	B
Yield to pressure	Pile on pressure
Make offers	Make threats
Trust others	Distrust others
Search for the single answer, the one they will accept	Hold out for the single answer, the one you will accept

Which is most like you – A or B?

Activity 20, *Asserting Yourself*, looks at how we behave with others – passively, aggressively or assertively. Simply put, passive behaviour allows others to walk all over us, aggressive behaviour means we walk all over others (and their rights), whereas assertive behaviour allows each of us to walk forward.

Applying this to negotiation, the soft negotiator wants to avoid conflict, and so readily makes concessions to reach agreement. However, as in a personal

relationship, they may end up feeling exploited. The hard negotiator sees the situation as a contest of wills, in which those who shout loudest and hold out longest fare best. Such archetypal aggressive behaviour may yield short-term gains, but over time is likely to damage relationships, and eventually isolate the aggressor.

A third way is both hard and soft, and assumes that you can obtain what you are entitled to and still behave decently. Here negotiation is approached and seen as a 'making' process, where the parties build and make an agreement with which all can live.

Step 2

The *principled negotiation* approach was developed by the Harvard Negotiation Project and is designed to produce agreements that are both fair and fully implementable. There are four principles:

1. *Separate the people from the problem*
   Go easy on the people but hard on the problem.
2. *Focus on interests, not positions*
   Explore mutual interests, rather than make offers or issue threats.
3. *Invent options for mutual gain*
   Designing good solutions under pressure is difficult. Adversarial situations tend to narrow vision and imagination. One way round this is to set aside an agreed period of time in which to develop a wide range of possible solutions that advance *shared interests*.
4. *Insist on objective criteria*
   An aggressive negotiator may try to get their way through intransigence. The assertive negotiator can insist that fair standards (e.g. market value, independent expert advice, health and safety regulations) are used.

Step 3

Think of a current or forthcoming negotiation. This might be at work – over scarce resources, a joint project, etc.; or at home – over holidays, childcare and so on. Choose a situation where the parties have roughly equal power (because dealings between people with very unequal power have a different flavour).

Thinking of your negotiation, use the four principles to analyse it as in Table A25.1. Jot down ideas for applying principled negotiation to your situation. A supportive friend will be helpful here.

Step 4

Preparation is always vital in negotiation. Make the time to develop your ideas before you meet the other party. If you are part of a team, set aside time to brainstorm the options for mutual gain.

Table A25.1 Four principles of negotiation

1 Separate the people from the problem	2 Focus on interests not positions	3 Invent options for mutual gain	4 Insist on objective criteria

This is good preparation in more than one sense, for it will often develop a sense of unity in a team. However, remember that you are inventing possibilities and options prior to working with the other party and not trying to reach firm decisions and make your mind up yet – stay loose.

Follow-up

This activity is based on one of the best and most straightforward books on negotiating and managing conflict – Roger Fisher and William Ury's *Getting to Yes* (Random House, 3rd edition, 2012). Roger Fisher has written many other books in this field, including, with co-author Daniel Shapiro, *Building Agreement: Using Emotions as You Negotiate* (Random House, 2007). He also provides the foreword in the broader *Difficult Conversations: How to Discuss What Matters Most*, by Douglas Stone, Bruce Patton and Sheila Heen (Penguin, 2000).

Collaborative Working

Managerial qualities	**People skills:** Emotional resilience: Creativity

Task forces, teams and partnerships have assumed greater importance with the increase in strategic alliances, joint ventures, collaborative projects and inter-agency working. All these joint efforts involve pooling resources, concentrating expertise and bringing together energy and effort across departmental and organizational boundaries. However, all projects have their difficulties and, as much of the effort always seems to go into the technical side, they often crop up on the social, interpersonal and political side.

Projects put a premium on collaborative work. Working with people with whom we have no formal responsibility or authority often leads to conflicts of loyalty where departments and project teams pull in different directions. Lack of clarity as to what to expect of each other can cause tension and frustration. Resentments, lack of cooperation and incomplete development of the project may arise if the practical issues of working together are not discussed and resolved. For collaborations to be effective, good 'rules of engagement' need to be established.

The following activity will help you prepare for collaborative working. Work through it by relating it to a specific project in which you are about to be involved.

Activity

Step 1

List all the things that you would be prepared to *share* in a collaborative working relationship. Here is the start of a possible list – to which you can add:

1.   Office space

2.   Administrative back-up

3.   Access to your equipment

4.   Your client files

5.   Your best ideas

6.   Your mobile phone

7.   Your favourite lunch venue

8.   Other resources

9.   and so on.

You could add certain provisos – 'will share office space as long as it's left tidy'.

Now make a list of the things you would *not* be willing to share – you might want to swap things from this list to your 'share' list, and again add items not mentioned:

1. Your professional networks and contacts

2. Your books

3. Your departmental budget

4. Your time outside work

5. and so on.

Step 2

When you have made your lists, ask yourself: *What are my worries about this project?*

Note these carefully. For example, consequences of failure, extra workload, concerns about particular team members, worries about disclosing know-how or information.

Step 3

Any collaborative project is a powerful learning opportunity. What learning goals could you accomplish via this project? Here are a few possible examples to start you off:

- ■ to widen my knowledge outside my professional field
- ■ to increase my visibility with senior people
- ■ to gain experience of other parts of the company/industry
- ■ to put myself into a high-risk situation
- ■ to improve my group working and management skills.

Now think about what you could *offer* to your partners. What knowledge, skills or personal qualities are you prepared to offer to other people on this project?

Step 4

Next think about the qualities you would like your project colleagues to have. Complete the following sentences:

What I want are people who *know* _____

_____

What I want are people who *can* _____

_____

What I want are people who *will* _____

_____

You could include standards of behaviour in this list. How should this person behave towards your staff, your boss, yourself? What actions will provoke resentment (e.g. borrowing things without asking, not listening to suggestions, using offensive language)?

While you are at it, is there any way you might need to moderate or change your own behaviour?

Step 5

Next, draft some ground rules in plain terms covering how you and the others can work together. These can cover any of the issues you have covered above, e.g.

Sample ground rules

- Work from a basic assumption of equality – in terms of ideas, rights, etc.
- Make time to listen to each other's ideas.
- Willingness to share resources in terms of administration, files, work space, etc.
- No smoking in work areas.
- Build in time for 'after action reviews' for learning purposes.
- Agree to refer disputes to an external facilitator/arbitrator.

Step 6

Finally, agree a joint set of ground rules at an early meeting with the whole project team. Keep this agreed list – perhaps pinned to the wall as a guide to good behaviour. From time to time you can review the ground rules together. Do they need revising? Do we need to add anything?

Follow-up

There are many sources on partnership working and collaborative advantage, often by specific industries such as construction or social work. For health, see, for example: http://www.dh.gov.uk/en/Publicationsandstatistics/Publications/PublicationsPolicyAndGuidance/DH_4003149.

Or from the Office for Fair Trading:

http://www.oft.gov.uk/about-the-oft/partnership-working/#.ULsZzoWBWUc.

David Archer and Alex Cameron's *Collaborative Leadership: How to Succeed in an Interconnected World* (Butterworth-Heinemann, 2009) constructs the idea under the more general headline of leadership, while Brian Littlechild and Roger Smith's edited title, *A Handbook for Inter-professional Practice in the Human Services* (Pearson, 2013), is aimed at students and practitioners looking to understand and develop better inter-agency working.

Be a Coach!

Managerial qualities	**People skills:** Professional knowledge and skills: Ability to learn

It is said that every *good* manager and leader is a coach. Think of the best manager you have ever had: did they make time to coach you?

In addition to helping other people, being a coach is also one of the best ways of learning for yourself: 'See one, do one, teach one', as the old surgeon's motto has it.

Questioning is at the heart of good coaching. This activity is based on the GROW model, which is perhaps the most widespread model used in this field. It is a framework and a checklist of the sorts of questions that a coach can use in coaching both individuals and teams. You can be a coach. You should be a coach for others and for yourself.

Activity

The questions offered in this activity can be used to start the coaching session, during the session to draw out the learning, clarify expectations and set goals, or after to summarize and review the learning.

Step 1

Find a friend or colleague who is prepared to be coached by you. It can be someone new to the organization or someone who is facing a tricky situation that they would like to think through.

Be open with this person about your own coaching skills. If this is new for you, then explain that you want to develop your skills in this area and learn about the coaching process. Explain how you are intending to go about it. Agree in advance that you will have a joint review session where you can get feedback from your partner on how helpful they found the process and how you could improve.

Step 2

Once you have a partner to be coached, agree a contract for three coaching sessions at regular intervals – weekly or monthly, for example.

Set times for these sessions and put them in your diaries. Allow an hour for each session.

Step 3

The coaching process is one of guided questioning to help the person move forward with their issue or situation. In your first session, follow the sequence of the GROW Model (Figure A27.1) in seeking to guide your partner through an exploration of the goal that they are trying to achieve, an evaluation of the options for action, and a testing of their commitment to achieve the goal:

G **GOAL** – *Setting goals for the task in general, or for this session.*
R **REALITY** – *Testing and raising awareness of the current situation.*
O **OPTIONS** – *Finding alternative strategies, solutions, answers and ways forward.*
W **WILL** – *Testing commitment to goals, and making concrete, realistic plans and steps to reach them.*

Complete the first coaching session in 50 minutes and keep the last 10 minutes for reviewing the effectiveness of the session with your partner.

Step 4

How did you do? What did you learn from the first coaching session?

If you ran out of questions or ideas, some further questions to help with each of the stages of the GROW model are given in Figure A27.2.

These questions are offered as a guide – nothing more. Use any that fit your natural style and language and do not slavishly follow the G–R–O–W sequence if it is not working.

The GROW Model: *Goal, Reality, Options, Will*

GOAL

- What is it you want to achieve?
- When you get there, what will it look like, sound like, and feel like?
- When you achieve this, what else will it help you to do?

REALITY

- What is happening at the moment?
- What are you dissatisfied about?
- What else is happening at the moment?
- Who is involved in the situation and what are they doing?
- What do you want to take forward from what is happening at present?

OPTIONS

- What options for action do you have?
- What else have you thought of (and rejected)?
- Have you thought of…?
- Do you have the resources to make the change?
- Who could help you in this?

WILL

- Which option do you most favour?
- How committed are you to taking this action (on a scale of 1–10)?
- What do you need to do to increase your will to do this?
- What support do you need?
- What is the first step you will take?
- When?

Figure A27.1 GROW model

GOAL

- What exactly do you want to achieve – short and long term?
- How will you know if you reach your goal?
- Is any part of it measurable?
- Why is the goal desirable, challenging and achievable for you?
- How would you rate your achievements so far, in this respect?
- How can you break down the goal into more manageable sub-goals?

REALITY

- Why haven't you reached this goal already?
- What have you done so far?
- What have you learnt from that?
- Who will there be the winners and losers if you get what you want?
- What is *really* stopping you?
- What constraints – *inside and outside yourself* – are holding you back?
- How might you overcome these?
- How might you sabotage your own efforts?

OPTIONS

- What else could you do? (Repeat this question until you both get fed up with it)
- What would you do if time and resources were not an issue?
- How could you change yourself so that it would not be less a problem?
- What would happen if you did nothing?
- Whom do you admire or respect who does this really well?
- What might this person do in your situation?

WILL

- How does this goal fit in with your other personal priorities?
- Which option(s) will you choose?
- How will that help you?
- What could possibly go wrong?
  (How will you overcome them?)
- Who else should know about your plan?
  (How will you inform them?)
- How committed are you really to this?
- If your commitment is low, might it be better to find something that you *really* want to do?
- What is Plan B?

Figure A27.2 Further GROW questions

If it seems to you that there is a better question arising from the situation or if it seems better to start with first steps and work backwards, try that out – whatever works for you and the other person.

Most of all coaching is a relationship and if the other person wants sympathy or clear direction, information or feedback, then go with that – as long as you feel it is appropriate.

Follow-up

Coaching is one of the most useful approaches to one-to-one management development and there are many books and websites available, many of them utilizing the GROW model or something similar. The Chartered Institute of Personnel and Development (CIPD) has free and useful factsheets on all aspects of HR, including coaching and mentoring: www.cipd.co.uk › HR Resources › Factsheets.

John Whitmore's *Coaching for Performance: Growing People, Performance and Purpose* (Nicholas Brealey, 4th edition, 2009) is a well-known book in this field. Also good are *Coaching and Mentoring at Work* by Mary Connor and Julia Pokora (Open University/McGraw-Hill, 2nd edition, 2012) and *Techniques for Coaching and Mentoring* by David Megginson and David Clutterbuck (Butterworth-Heinemann, 2005; Kindle Edition, 2012).

These last authors are involved in the European Mentoring and Coaching Council (EMCC), which brings together practitioners, researchers and institutions and is attempting to regulate this new profession: www.emccouncil.org.

The Follow-up references for Activity 5, *Find a Mentor*, might also be useful here.

Virtual Leadership

Managerial qualities	**People skills:** Professional knowledge and skills: Ability to learn

Are you faced with a new leadership challenge of virtual working? While virtual working has now arrived, many managers and leaders are still to come to terms with it.

How virtual is your world? You are now living in a virtual working environment if:

1. You and your colleagues spend a high proportion of your working time at a computer screen or workstation, interacting with others remotely, whether they be a few yards away or on the other side of the world.
2. Your organization works with, and relies on, a high degree of internal transparency over data and information, virtual teamwork and decision making, use of shared databases and devices.
3. Your organization relates in a virtual way to its external stakeholders – whether they be owners/sponsors, customers/clients, suppliers, employees, neighbours and all those whose lives are affected by its activities.

For example, Amazon and eBay interact with their users and customers almost entirely virtually. In the old days, the UK Lego salesmen went round corner shops taking orders; today the company distributes through supermarkets and negotiates the range and display of what they sell, while the point of sales tills track what is being sold, the stock rooms are automatically topped up from the warehouses, and the invoices follow on automatically.

The more these things are present, the more you are working in a virtual environment. Consider the following questions:

■ How do you find virtual working? How is it different from the way things used to be?
■ What do you like and dislike about it?
■ What are you able to cope with and what do you struggle with?

A new challenge

Virtual work and organization have been emerging for some time now, but research on the subject is relatively new. One as yet unresolved question is whether virtual working is like face-to-face working by another medium, or whether there is something new about it.

Often, according to Shoshana Zuboff (1985, 1988), the first thing we do with information technology is to 'automate' things – that is, do what we already do but perhaps more cheaply, quickly and reliably (though this is not to be counted on!). After the automation stage we may do something new and different with it, which she terms 'informating', which is rather like the 'transparency' mentioned above.

Virtual leadership is still currently in the 'automation' phase – traditional leadership in a new medium. But before too long something new will come along, and whoever gets there first will have a great idea for a new line in leadership development.

Activity

Table A28.1 provides the basis for a stock check of your current experience of virtual leadership and teamwork. For each statement fill out the three columns on the right, checking not only your current experience but also your views on whether this aspect is new and, if it is, what the implications are for your development and learning.

If you do not have much experience of virtual working, this will be more difficult. You could talk to other people you know who do. Or you could guess, or look at some of the data sources we offer later to see if you agree. As virtual working is likely to enter your world at some stage, this could be a worthwhile investment.

Table A28.1 The 24 Aspects of Virtual Leadership and Teamwork

The 24 Aspects	Is this true for you?	Is this new to virtual leadership and teamwork?	What are the implications of this factor for your virtual leadership development?
1. Virtual work and activity have the potential to contribute to eco efficiency, and leadership can help make this happen			
2. Virtual stuff is helping make inter-organizational alliances easier, and leadership is likely to have a role in making it happen and that there is something useful in it for the leader's employer			
3. Virtual teams may have more complex environments due partly to the dispersion of team members. Their members may have more loyalties and ties outside the team and the teams may tend to be 'explosive' rather than 'implosive' in network theory terms. Dealing with this is likely to be a new challenge to virtual team leaders			
4. Dealing with team members in multiple time zones can be a challenge. Asynchronous working (where people are not online together at the same time, but leave messages, be they an e-mail circulation or discussion space) may help, but it has its downsides too			
5. Some forms of virtual teamworking, particularly asynchronous, may help level the playing field for introverts and people who need more time to think			
6. Some forms of virtual teamworking may *increase* members' performance in listening – because they are aware of the challenge and try harder			
7. Virtual meetings may be more demanding and tiring and therefore need to be shorter or have more breaks in them, but this is not entirely clear			
8. Maintaining task alignment may be more challenging in virtual teams			
9. Virtual team leaders may need to negotiate their roles more explicitly, and this may apply to other team members too			

Table A28.1 (*continued*)

The 24 Aspects	Is this true for you?	Is this new to virtual leadership and teamwork?	What are the implications of this factor for your virtual leadership development?
10. There are choices for virtual teams and their leaders over high- or low-tech resources. Low-tech has a lot going for it			
11. Virtual team leaders' values and attitudes appear to be easier to pick up by members, as are inconsistencies in them			
12. Performance in areas like speed of response to communications is more obvious, which has good and bad implications			
13. Similarly some virtual exchanges leave more of a record, which can be good or bad. Virtual teams can be trapped by the rear view mirror effect			
14. Virtual team members' patience in reading background documents appears to be more limited than in face-to-face groups			
15. There are issues to do with body language and subtle signals for virtual teams			
16. The performance of virtual teams is likely to be affected more by the background organizational structure relationships between members, or to put it another way, they may need more egalitarian relations to be effective, though this is by no means clear-cut			
17. Because virtual teams can be more dispersed, there might be greater ethnic and cultural differences to deal with			
18. Virtual teams may need to be more aware of, and deal more explicitly with, boundaries of all kinds			
19. Establishing trust early on is important			
20. Prior face-to-face meetings may be appreciated but are not necessary			
21. Time for informal and spontaneous chat is important			

(*continued*)

Table A28.1   *(continued)*

The 24 Aspects	Is this true for you?	Is this new to virtual leadership and teamwork?	What are the implications of this factor for your virtual leadership development?
22. Traditional teleconferencing etiquette (e.g. one person talks at a time, clear moderation) may not be appropriate in the early trust forming stage			
23. A more dialogical rather than debating style of conversation is appropriate at least at the more exploratory stages, i.e. more clarifying and building on ideas rather than defending and attacking lines of argument			
24. Some of the more manipulative dysfunctional political behaviours that occur in face-to-face teams are more difficult in virtual teams			

How did you fare with this stock take? The 24 Aspects of Virtual Leadership and Teamwork offer glimpses of what is new and emerging in the world of virtual organization, work, teams and leadership.

Conclusion: what is the future for virtual leadership?

The most obvious impact of this new environment is that we increasingly work in and lead virtual teams. For example, one of us worked with Exxon Research who, just a few years ago, relocated whole teams and their families to different research centres in America, England or Germany. It was both expensive and calamitous when things went wrong. Today, team members stay where they are, meet occasionally for a two- or three-day meeting, and work virtually for the rest of the time.

Beyond virtual teamwork, what is emerging is still somewhat obscure and its features have not as yet been codified. Some of the answers to the question, *What is the future for virtual leadership?*, may be found in the current practices of those organizations – the Amazons, Googles, e-Bays and Facebooks – that were born in and are of the virtual era. They do seem to be different in various ways. For example, as we can see, they are rarely on the client lists of Business Schools. Perhaps they do not find Business School leadership development offerings relevant to them?

Another way in which they are different is that few, if any, of them have faced the obsolescence of their core ideas. Are virtually based businesses led by big ideas rather than by dominant individuals? Virtual leadership here seems to involve creative visualization and systems design. Apple seems to have been good at spotting good ideas and having their core strength in creative and aesthetic design, which has commanded a premium in terms of price.

The importance of design extends to the IT system and its delivery infrastructures. Perhaps these systems themselves then deliver distributed leadership. Virtual bookshops, marketplaces and social networks often display a widely distributed leadership.

So our feeling is that this move to virtual working and leadership is more fundamental than the simple 'automation' of existing practices. We suspect that there is something bigger or more fundamental going on. Let's watch this space together. To join a discussion on this, contact: j.burgoyne@lancaster.ac.uk.

Follow-up

The Follow-up sources for *The Virtual Revolution* (Activity 37) would also be useful here.

References

Zuboff, S. (1985) 'Automate/informate: two faces of intelligent technology', *Organisational Dynamics*, 14(2): 5–18.

Zuboff, S. (1988) *In the Age of the Smart Machine.* London: Heinemann.

The Saturated Life

Managerial qualities	**Emotional resilience:** Self-knowledge

Are you overloaded?

There are few people in management and leadership roles who don't feel busy, stretched and overloaded. We are overloaded not just by tasks and demands on our time, but by stimuli, information, data – messages of all kinds.

Kenneth Gergen coined the phrase 'the saturated self' to label this phenomenon in which we are battered by demands to be and do things. The information/message overload does not just create work in itself; it makes demands on our emotions, sense of self and identity.

Messages give us information and make demands on us to respond, to do something. They communicate other people's expectations of us, including telling us how to be (as in advertising). 'Active load' consists of messages passed directly to us: information, knowledge, expectations, response demands; 'passive load', like passive smoking, includes advertising, publicity, propaganda and unsolicited communications of all kinds.

The load problem is to do with how much we can cope with in processing terms. But more than that, these are demands on our energy, emotions, sense of self, image and reputation. The active and passive loads can exert many conflicting demands that exhaust us, cause us to distort things and become internalized as problems.

Activity

Step 1: Getting the feel of your message load

Make some notes on your active and passive message loads now, compared with some time ago – when you were growing up, or starting work. Think of your active load now: e-mails, phone messages, phone calls, paperwork and meetings. Think of your passive load: news, advertising, hoardings, labels, noticeboards.

	Active load	Passive load
Now		
Before		

Step 2: Exploring your message load

Think about the following, and write a few notes on them:

(a) What are the times and where are the places where your 'message load' comes to you?

_____

_____

_____

(b) Do you stimulate or inhibit the message load that you get? Are you select-ive about how you do this?

_____

_____

_____

(c) Some people are 'stimulus addicts' – they set themselves up for a continu-ous flow of messages to save thinking, addressing priorities, facing up to problems. Can you detect any signs of this in yourself?

_____

_____

_____

Step 3: Things to do about it

Consider your answers to the following questions:

(a) What do you do to manage the active message demand on you? Do you have an approach to influencing the sources of messages to give you just what you want – not too much, not too little?

_____

_____

_____

(b) Do you manage the passive message demand on you? Do you limit the amount of advertising, general news, notices that you allow to take your attention? How?

_____

_____

_____

(c) Do you create breathing spaces, places and times where you are not exposed to messages, have time to reflect, get back in touch with yourself and priorities? When?

_____

_____

_____

(d) Or the other side of this coin, do you limit the times and places that messages can get to you, and control when and where you deal with them? How?

_____

_____

_____

(e) Do you have a way of being selective about the messages that reach you, and the degree of urgency with which they do so? How?

_____

_____

_____

(f) Are you proactive in arranging for your messages to be at the right level of summarization for you, e.g. executive summaries rather than full reports, headline statistics not masses of data?

_____

_____

_____

(g) Can you be comfortable 'not knowing' about some things – trusting others to deal with them, or tell you if anything exceptional or unusual comes up?

_____

_____

_____

(h) Can you avoid just being a messenger – passing on information that does not really have to come through you – by arranging for it to pass you by and go directly to where it is needed?

_____

_____

_____

(i) In some workplaces, people seem to get into competitive and dysfunctional games of swamping and drowning each other in messages – consciously or unconsciously. Are you caught up in this? How can you avoid it?

_____

_____

_____

(j) Do you take enough time to 'collect yourself and your thoughts' – to work out what you are doing and what information you actually need, as opposed to get?

_____

_____

_____

(k) Do you consider the message load on others – identifying and understanding their problems and situations, and what you do to increase or decrease it?

_____

_____

_____

(l)   There are many positive aspects of living in an information-demand-rich world – are you skilled in using it to find out what you want, rather than being swamped by it?

_____

_____

_____

Follow-up

The core idea for this activity is in Kenneth Gergen's _The Saturated Self: Dilemmas of Identity in Contemporary Life_ (Basic Books, 1991), but if this aspect of managerial life is a concern for you, there are many self-help books on how to stop worrying, most of them rather simplistic. Robert Leahy's _The Worry Cure: Stop Worrying and Start Living_ (Piatkus, 2006) takes a Cognitive Behaviour Therapy approach to this perennial problem. Both scholarly and practical, the book is full of stories and ideas for helping overcome anxiety and making changes in positive directions.

Mind, the mental health charity, has an excellent website offering information and help of various kinds, including the address of local groups: http://www.mind.org.uk/.

Difficult Situations

Managerial qualities	**Emotional resilience:** Analytical skills

We all face 'difficult situations' at times in our work and in our personal lives. A difficult situation is one in which (i) something important is at stake, (ii) things are not going right or (iii) where there seems to be no obvious way forward: situations in which you feel 'in a corner' or 'between a rock and a hard place'.

For example, it may be a target that you can see no way of meeting, but one that you will be punished for if you fail. Or, you may find yourself falling out with someone you want to get on well with, or find that an esteemed colleague that you do not want to offend is doing something of which you deeply disapprove. And so on; there are lots of difficult situations.

How do you cope in situations like this?

It may or may not be a comfort to remember that in seemingly impossible situations that nothing stays the same for ever, that there is a future, that something else will happen. The thing to worry about is how to cope and how to shape this new situation. As Friedrich Nietzsche said, 'that which does not kill me makes me strong' – emotional resilience is built by learning to cope with adversity.

Five options for difficult situations

There are five ways out of a difficult situation: love it, leave it, live with it, change it or change yourself.

■ *Love it* – this means asking yourself why you are so concerned about the difficult situation – what makes you stick in there and try to deal with it – if

we really think about it we may find some core of ourselves that finds it worthwhile to struggle with this one – the struggle is the measure of our caring. It may also be possible (probably sometimes not always) to 'reframe' the situation in a more positive light – the breaking down of something may give the opportunity to re-build it in a more positive way.

■ *Leave it* – on the other hand, do you want to stick in there with it? Why not just walk away? Does it have to be your problem? What exactly are the costs of getting out of it? Might they be less than the costs of staying with it? Are there some benefits to walking away from it? A more constructive use of your energies?

■ *Live with it* – which is what we are doing while we work out what to do. Can you just go on like this? What actually happens if you do nothing? What is the worst that can happen? Are there any defensive moves you can make to lessen the pain while leaving it alone? Things and situations do change – if you do nothing, it is possible that things will right themselves of their own accord, even if it seems difficult to imagine how they might do so now. Sometimes anything you might do has a greater chance of making things worse rather than better, so why not leave it alone?

■ *Change it* – let's look at it one more time – what would it actually take to deal with the situation? If you had a magic wand, what would you do? Is it that other people do not see that there is a problem, or see it the same way we do? What would it take to tell them and ask them to help us change it? Do you need to be more assertive in this situation? Are you being creative enough in your search for solutions? What would the most effective and successful person you know do with this situation?

■ *Change yourself* – is the situation difficult because you are hanging on to some idea of yourself – as competent, respected, popular or something else? These things may be very special for us and non-negotiable, but maybe not. Can you make the difficulty reduce or go away by changing your idea of who you are or who you want to be?

Activity

Use this framework to think about difficult situations in your life – past, present and future. This activity is simply a thought experiment – applying these ideas to difficult situations that you have, and might face in the future.

Past

Think of the most difficult situation that you have faced in the past:

■ Which of the five avenues did you take or try?
■ What worked?

- ■ What did not work for you?
- ■ Which did you try first and which did you try later?
- ■ How did you resolve it in the end?

Present

What is the most difficult situation facing you now? Think about what each of the options looks like for this.

- ■ Which do you rule out and why?
- ■ Which is the best or least bad of them?
- ■ What can you do to make it more acceptable?

Future

Is there a particularly difficult situation coming your way?

If not, what general kinds of difficulty do you think might come up for you in the future? Can you think of ways of setting things up so that at least one of the five options will work for you?

Conclusion

Looking back over this activity, do you have a general habit or pattern in how you deal with difficult situations?

For example, are you always trying to change other people when it may not be realistic? Or, are you always trying to escape from difficulties? Does this get you into trouble? Should you try to broaden your repertoire of coping approaches?

Follow-up

A little philosophy may help in such difficult situations. Try the master in a well-translated version: Friedrich Nietzsche's *Why I Am So Wise* is translated by Gerta Valentine (Chartwell Books, 2009). At the other end of the scale, Karl Stalb's website offers quick solutions to 16 difficult situations at work: http://www.workhappynow.com/2010/03/16-difficult-office-situations/.

Are You Stressed?

Managerial qualities	**Emotional resilience:** Self-knowledge

Stress-related illnesses are a major killer of leaders, managers and professional workers. More than a century ago, we learned that the inhalation of dust and fumes led to lung disease and silicosis. We are now learning what causes coronary heart disease, cancer and strokes, and it is increasingly obvious that these diseases are related to the way we live and work. This includes what we eat, how much we exercise, how much tension and pressure we experience, and how we handle them.

Looking after ourselves is not just about avoiding an early grave, because the killers head an unpleasant list of usually non-fatal ailments, including arthritis, asthma, chronic anxiety, colitis, diabetes, eczema, hypertension, mental illness, neurosis, migraines and many other symptoms of physical, emotional and mental distress.

How are you feeling so far? This is not a pretty picture and it's not surprising that many of us close our eyes to it.

This activity starts with a short questionnaire on how you behave at work.

Activity

Step 1: Work Habits Questionnaire

How are you at work? Relaxed, tolerant and easy-going? Or are you tense, easily frustrated and irritable?

Circle the number on each scale in Table A31.1 that best characterizes your *usual* response or behaviour at work; that is, 1 or 5 if you are *very* like the behaviour described at that end; 2 or 4 if you lean towards that end; and 3 if you genuinely feel in the middle.

Table A31.1   **Work Habits Questionnaire**

uncompetitive, avoid conflict	1	2	3	4	5	highly competitive, I like battles
do things at an easy pace	1	2	3	4	5	do things quickly (walk, eat, drive, etc.)
feel as though there's always plenty of time	1	2	3	4	5	feel as though there's never enough time
have many hobbies and interests	1	2	3	4	5	am only interested in work, I talk a lot about work
always do one thing at a time	1	2	3	4	5	usually keep several balls in the air at once
never hurry	1	2	3	4	5	am always rushing about, always in a hurry
take time off to relax and to think things over	1	2	3	4	5	feel guilty about taking time off to relax
am casual about timekeeping	1	2	3	4	5	am never late

TOTAL SCORE . . . _____ (sum of all the ringed numbers)

Step 2

This questionnaire is based on the work of two cardiologists, Friedman and Rosenman (1974), who have suggested that certain types of behaviour are much more likely to lead to coronary heart disease. A composite of these gives us the 'Type A' person, who is:

- very competitive
- continually striving for achievement
- forever in a hurry
- liable to explosive outbursts of 'free floating aggression'
- tense, pressurized, urgent, 'hyped up'.

By contrast, the 'Type B' person is:

- relaxed
- able to play without guilt

- able to become absorbed in books, entertainments, conversations and other non-work interests
- not easily irritated, frustrated or angered
- in little need of displaying achievements.

Step 3: Scoring

If you scored between:

- 8 and 15 then you're a definite 'Type B' person
- 16 and 23 then you lean towards the 'Type B' person
- exactly 24 then you're well balanced between the two
- 25 and 32 then you lean towards 'Type A'
- 33 and 40 they you're definitely 'Type A'.

An absolute 'Type B' person would be so 'laid back' that leading and managing activities would either be impossible or not worth the trouble! The important point is that much of this sort of work reinforces any natural tendencies we have and actually *requires* 'Type A' behaviours. We are rewarded for displaying them. This is the main way in which such work forms us – or rather, deforms us.

Follow-up

To start treating yourself better, see the next activity, *Treat Yourself Well*.

There are lots of online materials on stress and related issues. You could do worse than to start with the Health & Safety Executive, which offers many resources, including e-bulletins, research reports, video cases and links to other useful websites: http://www.hse.gov.uk/stress/resources.htm.

There are also many books available Here are two: *A Guide to Managing Workplace Stress* by Trevor Hicks and Caroline McSherry (Dissertation.com, 2007) and *The Work-Place Stress Survival Guide* by Annette Young (Kindle edition, 2012), which is only available as a Kindle book but is very cheap and provides a simple way to identify the different types of stress, and gives quick and easy advice on how to manage it.

Reference

Friedman, M. and Rosenman, R.H. (1974) *Type-A Behavior and Your Heart*. New York: Knopf.

Treat Yourself Well

Managerial qualities	**Emotional resilience:** Self-knowledge

Leaders get attacked, dismissed, silenced and sometimes assassinated because they come to represent loss.

Ronald Heifetz

Leadership work can be dangerous and stressful. There are times when you are *the* woman or man in charge and you have to take the blame or 'flak', often on behalf of others or for the organization as a whole. This is part of the territory.

As we saw in the previous activity, this can lead to a highly stressed lifestyle, which can kill or disable you if you do not take care of yourself.

Activity

Some of the best ways of avoiding the worst effects of leadership and managerial work are to do with building up your inner strength with healthy habits.

Step 1: Healthy habits

Tick any of the following that you do habitually and add any of your own at the end.

1. I build up resistance by regular sleep, a healthy diet and plenty of exercise.
2. I talk problems through with my partner.

3. I talk problems through with my boss or colleagues.
4. I practise meditation or relaxation.
5. I withdraw physically from stressful situations when I can.
6. I block out one day or half a day per month in my diary just to spend exactly as I want.
7. I allow myself a good read every day with a novel that takes all my attention.
8. I give myself breaks and treats when I need them.
9. I practise being quiet and avoid being the centre of attention.
10.
11.
etc.

Score one point for each of 1–9 that you ticked. Score two points for each of 10 onwards.

If you scored more than seven points, you may become stressed on occasions, but at least you do have some ways of giving yourself a break now and then.

If you scored less than seven points, don't you think you should be doing something about this?

Step 2: Treats

Treats are the rewards and gifts you give yourself. 'I'll just have a little something now' you say, and quite right too. Many busy managers and leaders come to over-rely on particular sources of 'treats' – especially alcoholic drinks after work – and being able to treat yourself properly is about taking care of yourself in all sorts of ways. This includes an ability to reward and pamper yourself at appropriate times – at the end of a hard day, in the middle of a knotty problem, when all seems gloomy and hopeless. Treats are usually little things that give great pleasure – taking a break, a walk in the park, phoning a friend, and so on.

The secret of managing stress successfully is being able to 'pleasure' yourself without guilt in many different ways. Does that sound a bit self-indulgent? Even indecent? Well, that is a problem. The Victorian work ethic encouraged people to split off their enjoyment and pleasures in life and keep them apart from the stern rectitude and selfless duty required at work. Some of us seem to have inherited this guilt about enjoying ourselves at work.

If you want to work hard and continue to enjoy rather than to destroy yourself, you need to take your pleasures seriously: *there is no incompatibility between enjoyment and productivity!*

Write down at least five ways in which you take care of yourself at work and treat yourself well:

1.

_____

_____

2.

_____

_____

3.

_____

_____

4.

_____

_____

5.

_____

_____

Were you able to manage that?

If not, why not? Women managers and leaders may often be juggling work, career development and family commitments and may not have the time or energy to treat themselves. Some men are bad at treating themselves and rely on women to be the 'emotional specialists' – and so on.

What's your pattern?

It might be good fun to do some research among your friends or colleagues. If you can enquire in the right spirit, it may throw up a surprising catch – there are all sorts of possibilities for treating yourself.

Follow-up

The resources for the previous activity, *Are You Stressed*, are also of relevance here, and the next two Activities will also help you with this quest. Take care.

Relaxation

Managerial qualities	**Emotional resilience**

It is said that when humans first evolved and were constantly faced with threats from dangerous animals, warring bands, and so on, the reactions of *fight* or *flight* became normal. The human body (like that of animals) prepares itself for threat in various physiological ways, including increased breathing rate, raised blood pressure, a faster heart beat and a greater flow of blood to muscles.

Managers and leaders, finding themselves under threat, may also resort to fight or flight and, although their stressful situations are very different from those of our ancestors, the body's response is similar.

Unfortunately, these body responses, although excellent for dealing with wild beasts, don't help much in coping with organizational problems. As we usually don't actually fight or run, all the physiological changes are channelled into other effects, causing irritable behaviour and stress and, in the longer term, these can accumulate with serious and lasting consequences.

To cope with the physical symptoms, some people in stressful jobs resort to prescription drugs. However, these can hardly be recommended as a long-term solution; what is needed is an internal method of coping with stress reactions. There are many, both ancient and modern, approaches to managing your own stress, often associated with specific philosophies or religions, such as the many forms of yoga and meditation.

The activity here is not associated with any particular belief system, but is a synthesis of the common elements of a number of approaches to relaxation. More than with most of the Activities in this book, you need to repeat this activity over a long period of time for it to work well.

Activity

Step 1

Find a quiet place where you can sit comfortably in your own space. It is important to be fairly straight and upright. Although some people like to sit cross-legged on the floor, this is not essential and you may be more comfortable in a chair. In this case, sit with both feet on the ground, back straight, head up. Don't be *too* comfortable – don't fall asleep.

Step 2

When you are comfortable, close your eyes and consciously relax all your muscles, starting at the top of your head and moving down through your body to the tips of your toes. Do this gradually, trying to sense each part of the body and muscle groups.

If you have difficulty in doing this, tell yourself that you're becoming more and more relaxed, that you are going deeper . . . and deeper . . . and deeper. It is often helpful to imagine yourself going down, in a lift, on an escalator; in warm water, to the bottom of the sea.

Step 3

Breathe through your nose, and listen to your own breathing. As you become more relaxed, you will notice your breathing become slower, shallower and more restful. Note that at the bottom of each breath (i.e. after breathing out), there is a pause before you begin to breathe in again.

Step 4

When you have noticed these pauses, start counting backwards from ten to one. Count thus: breathe out, TEN, breathe in; breathe out, NINE, breathe in; breathe out, EIGHT, breathe in, etc. Count in this way from ten down to one, then back up from one to ten, down from ten to one, and so on.

Step 5

Stray thoughts may come into your head while you are breathing/counting. Don't worry about – just let the thought come, don't dwell on it, let it go. Then go back to TEN and start counting again. Don't worry if you never reach ONE, especially in the early days.

Step 6

Continue breathing/counting in this way for 15–20 minutes (although 10 minutes may be easier to start with) at least once a day, though twice is better. Keep a watch or clock handy, and check if you wish (otherwise keep your eyes closed). When you finish, remain sitting quietly for a few minutes before standing up slowly.

Follow-up

This activity is one that should be incorporated into your lifestyle to be of maximum benefit.

You might like to carry the simple technique given in this activity a stage further. There are numerous books, tapes, aromatic oil kits and all sorts of wonderful things that aim to help you to relax. Matthew Johnson's *Quiet the Mind* (Pan Macmillan, 2011) is a very simple and calming text that comes with pictures to help you develop the practice of dealing with the unquiet mind. Mark Williams and Danny Penman's *Mindfulness: An Eight-week Plan for Finding Peace in a Frantic World* (Piatkus, 2011) is already a bestseller in the ancient and recently popular pursuit of mindfulness.

Fitness

Managerial qualities	**Emotional resilience**

There is a widely recognized link between physical fitness and mental alertness, high motivation and overall effectiveness. To be the manager or leader that you really can be, you need to keep yourself fit.

In this activity, we stress the importance of this aspect of self-development, and make some suggestions about the sources of further guidance.

Fashions in fitness come and go, and new books reflecting these ideas appear regularly. Find a regime of regular exercise that suits you – your personality, lifestyle, age, present level of fitness, and so on – and build it into your work and life. This will not only make you feel physically better, it will have a payoff in all areas of your work – particularly when you are in stressful, demanding situations. Put it this way: can you afford not to be fit?

There are many simple ways to improve your fitness – one US study showed that executives who climbed just 50 steps each day reduced their risk of heart disease by almost half. Climbing stairs and avoiding the lifts, walking two miles each day, going for a swim twice a week – all will make a difference. Just start doing something.

Follow-up

Walking is good for you – it's official! The British Government supports the Ramblers Association in organizing health walks at: http://www.walkingfor health.org.uk/.

At the other end of the scale, *The Official British Army Fitness Guide* by Sam Murphy (Guardian Books, 2009) is the standard text for would-be squaddies.

Finally, Activity 38, *Be Your Own Personal Trainer*, will give you plenty of ideas for getting fitter.

Manage Your Feelings

Managerial qualities	**Emotional resilience:** People skills: Self-knowledge

Being aware of our own feelings helps us to become more emotionally resilient. Awareness is a first requirement for control, and bottling up natural feelings – keeping a stiff upper lip – is not always a good thing.

Open expression of feelings can be beneficial to the individual and can lead to more open interpersonal relationships. This must be qualified. If you are just 'dumping' anger or distress on others or if there are strong organizational norms that make such expression taboo, this is unlikely to have good outcomes. We express feelings by what we say, but also significant is the way we say it, and the non-verbal means of facial expression, gesture and posture.

This activity offers an opportunity to practise at becoming aware of, and expressing, your feelings – and also at identifying the feelings as expressed by others. The aim is to have choice in how you handle your feelings. To bottle up or to freely express? These alternatives may be appropriate to particular situations; but if you bottle up your feelings, you'll have to express them somehow, somewhere. It is best by far that you are in charge of this expression.

Activity

Do Steps 1 and 2 with a partner – a colleague, spouse or friend, or even a small group of four or five persons.

Step 1

This focuses on the expression of feelings through the *way we speak*, as opposed to *what we say*.

Copy this list of feelings on to small cards or pieces of paper – one feeling per piece.

Excited	Patronizing	Angry
Depressed	Sarcastic	Bored
Happy	Tired	Affectionate
Enthusiastic	Disliking	Frightened
Threatened	Curious	Superior
Preoccupied	Cautious	Interested

Now shuffle the cards and select one at random. Imagine that your partner has just said or done something that evokes in you the feeling on the card. Get into that feeling and then demonstrate it in how you say the following:

Well, now, there are lots of implications in this.

Your partner now guesses what feeling you are trying to convey. If they get it wrong, try again.

Take it in turns to express and guess feelings. Do this for at least five rounds.

Now discuss this experience. Were some feelings particularly easy or difficult to express? Why do you think this is? How accurate were you and your partner in interpreting feelings? What are the implications of your answers?

Step 2

Now try the same activity, this time with the non-verbal expression of feelings, such as by facial expression, gesture, body posture, etc.

Follow the same procedure as for Step 1, except that instead of expressing feelings through the sentence, 'Well, now, there are lots of implications in this', do so in any way you wish but *without words.*

As before, take turns and then discuss.

Step 3

Use Table A35.1 to keep a 'feelings log' from your everyday activities. Examine the feelings you experience from events at work and identify how you *think* you expressed them, then check this out with the other people who were present.

Table A35.1 **The feelings log**

1 Your feelings at a particular time	2 What caused these feelings?	3 Did you express your feelings?	4 If not, why not? If so, how did you express them?	5 Check with others. How did they think you were feeling? Why?

Think of some events – meetings, discussions, episodes – from the last few weeks. Write down your feelings on each particular occasion in Column 1, then think about why you felt that way, and note that briefly in Column 2.

In Column 3, answer yes or no to the question, 'Did you express your feelings?' Explain your decision to express your feelings or not in Column 4. Finally, use Column 5 to check with the other people involved in the situation whether they correctly perceived your feelings or not. Ask them what *they* thought you were feeling, and why. Compare this with your own perception of your feelings, and the way in which you did or did not express them.

When you have made a number of entries in the feelings log, look for patterns or repeating themes. Ask yourself the following questions:

- Do certain types of events lead to certain feelings?
- What different causes lead to a particular feeling?
- Which feelings do I express, and which do I not?
- Why?

- When do I express feelings? When don't I?
- To whom do I express them? To whom don't I?
- Do people sense some of my feelings, but not others?
- Are some people more accurate in their perception of my feelings than others?

Follow-up

A great deal of attention has recently been given to the idea of 'emotional intelligence' and this has emerged as an important area of capability for managers and leaders. Daniel Goleman's *Emotional Intelligence* (Bantam Books, 2005) is relevant here but there are many other more recent texts. There are also useful websites: to test your EIQ (Emotional Intelligence Quotient), try MySkillsProfile. com, while The Emotional Intelligence Consortium (www.eiconsortium.org/) specializes in information and research related to the workplace.

Gael Lindenfield is a prolific author in the area of managing feelings. She presents a seven-step strategy for dealing with difficult or overwhelming feelings in *The Emotional Healing Strategy: A Recovery Guide for Any Setback, Disappointment or Loss* (Michael Joseph, 2008).

Stability Zones

Managerial qualities	**Emotional resilience**

The limits of emotional resilience are experienced as loss of control or ability to cope. We can all cope with huge amounts of change, pressure, complexity and confusion, as long as we have what Alvin Toffler called 'stability zones'. These are oases of balance and security in our lives that serve as anchors or retreats to allow us to cope with the chaos and instability of other areas.

Stability zones can be **Ideas**, **Places**, **People**, **Things** or **Organizations**. Working out where *your* stability zones are (or could be) – and then cultivating them – will develop your emotional resilience and capacity to cope with pressure.

■ **Ideas** may be deeply felt religious beliefs, or a strong commitment to a particular philosophy, political ideology, or cause.

■ **Places** as stability zones can be large-scale (like your country) or small-scale (like your street or room). These are your personal spaces where you feel at home, perhaps where you grew up or spent happy times.

■ Particular **People** provide a main source of stability for many of us. These are valued and enduring relationships with family members, long-standing friends or trusted colleagues.

■ **Things** as stability zones are favourite, familiar and comforting possessions. These can be clothes – that old shirt or pair of shoes – family heirlooms, items from childhood, treasured gifts or mementoes. **Things** can also be houses or books or cars. Lots of things.

- **Organizations** that provide stability include the work organization itself, professional bodies, membership institutes, clubs, communities of practice – any form of organizational belonging with which we identify.

Many stability zones overlap categories: home, for example, combines place, people, things and organizations. Given one good stability zone, we can cope with many sources of change and instability.

Activity

Work through the following questions, noting down your answers.

Step 1: What are YOUR stability zones?

Think through each of the five areas of ideas, places, things, people and organizations. Note specific anchors where you find stability under:

- Ideas?

_____

_____

_____

- Places?

_____

_____

_____

- People?

_____

_____

_____

- Things?

_____

_____

_____

    ■ Organizations?

_____

_____

_____

Step 2: How stable are your stability zones?

Look through your stability zones from Step 1. Are they sound and secure? Can you count on them staying the same? Will they last?

    ■ Ideas?
    ■ Places?
    ■ People?
    ■ Things?
    ■ Organizations?

Step 3: How satisfied are you with your stability zones?

Work through the following and make a few notes:

    ■ Are the ideas, places, things, people and organizations that you depend on enough for you?

_____

_____

_____

    ■ Are there any changes you want to make in your stability zones?

_____

_____

_____

    ■ Do you need to find some new ones?

_____

_____

_____

■ How could you work to develop your ideas, look after your possessions, care better for the people who are important to you?

_____

_____

_____

Follow-up

The idea of personal stability zones for 'coping with tomorrow' originates in Alvin Toffler's *Future Shock* (Pan, 1973).

MindTools (http://www.mindtools.com/pages/article/newTCS_90.htm) has an up-to-date briefing on this idea and lists lots of resources and papers on the topic.

Ed Schein has written several books and workbooks, including *Career Anchors* (Pfeiffer, 3rd edition, 2006), which are helpful for sorting out the important elements and values in your career.

The Virtual Revolution

Managerial qualities	**Emotional resilience:** Sensitivity to events: People skills: Analytical skills

Our world is now saturated with electronic communications, and the *virtual revolution* is said to be the most significant since the eighteenth-century industrial revolution in terms of how it affects society, the economy and how our own lives are structured. This revolution is transforming how we work and live.

There are three aspects to the virtualization of business, organizations and work:

- Virtual workplaces – the extent of work now done through e-mail, websites, the Internet and intranets, teleworking, dispersed teams, remote relationships, and so on.
- Virtual organizational dynamics – many organizational processes now work virtually – access to organizational members, information, resources; the monitoring of work relationships and personal performance; the functioning of value chains and networks, procurement and delivery of goods and services, including the management of intellectual and knowledge products, is done through IT-mediated relationships and systems in a virtually transparent world.
- Virtually located organizations – these are increasingly 'present' in the world through websites, portals and search engines. Organizations are increasingly electronically connected to suppliers, customers, clients and owners/sponsors.

Those who survive and thrive in this era will be those who understand it best and have the personal strategies to deal with it. Here are some ideas to help you into this position.

Step 1: Reviewing your virtual workstyle

Leaders and managers have been to some extent 'office workers', but the office is changing dramatically. Here is a progression of 'office types' – how are you situated now?

1. Private or shared office.
2. Open plan – fixed work space in a large room, with or without partitions and bookable private meeting rooms.
3. Hot desking – no fixed personal location, but temporary workspaces at particular locations – often with a personal mobile set of drawers and lap-top docking stations.
4. Café society-style workplaces, with an emphasis on informal meeting spaces – perhaps combined with hot desking.
5. Telecottaging – home-based workstation connected to the organizational intranets, etc.
6. Hypermobile workstyle – mobile working from wherever – trains, planes, cars, hotel foyers, other people's offices, cybercafés, etc.

The rationales for different office arrangements are influenced by fashion and status, as well as efficiency. Many senior managers still have more traditional offices (although sometimes combined with other types).

Consider the following questions:

1. What has been the history or pattern of office arrangements over your career?

2. What changes would you like to make to your current arrangements?

3. Do you have a working understanding of all the office arrangements listed above? Do you have the appropriate skills to work with all of them?

You need to be versatile in the kinds of arrangements that you are comfortable with, and can work effectively in.

Step 2: *Reviewing your virtual work relationships*

How adapted are you to the virtual processes and interactions within your organizations, including your relationships with other people and your access to resources?

Here are some questions to help review this:

1. Who and what do you work with in your organizational setting?

2. What is the mix of face-to-face and virtual interaction?

3. What virtual organizational processes are you hooked into (virtual meetings, overseeing IT-controlled business processes, working on virtual projects, etc.)?

4. How are these changing – for example, what is the trend to increasing virtualization in your organization?

5. Where does this leave you – are you being marginalized, or are trends making you more central to key organizational processes?

6. What organizational knowledge/information resources do you use, maintain, contribute to?

7. What is happening in terms of the virtualization of your organization's location? Is this expanding or obliterating your personal job/work/role?

Organizations are now 'known' in virtual space through websites and other virtual communication processes. Organizational location is increasingly virtualized and some organizations, such as e-retailers, exist almost entirely in virtual space, selling, delivering and being supplied through electronic management.

Step 3: Positioning yourself

To prepare for the virtual world, look at the following 'To Do' list. Tick any items that apply to you:

- Learn more about what's going on in terms of the further virtualization of my work and my organization.
- Acquire new skills including language/terminology, fluency with packages, on-line and web conferences, databases, etc.
- Get access to more resources including kit, maintenance help and back-ups, advice, education and learning opportunities.
- Get better and more connections to websites, intranets, special resources, etc.
- Up my virtual presence – get better represented on intranets, websites, etc., so others can find me.
- Make sure that I'm not in danger of being 'disintermediated', i.e. replaced as a go-between by search engines and websites, etc.

If you have ticked one or more items on this list, then print it off and carry it around with you until you have completed these tasks.

Follow-up

Much has been written about virtual teams and virtual working over the past few years. *Leading Virtual Teams* (Harvard Business School Press, 2010) is a short but authoritative guide to this increasingly common mode of managerial work. Another good book is Ghislaine Caulat's *Virtual Leadership: Learning to Lead Differently* (Libri Publishing, 2012), which highlights the importance of relational skills in the virtual environment.

The Follow-up resources from *Networking* (Activity 2) may also be useful here.

Be Your Own Personal Trainer

Managerial qualities	**Emotional resilience:** Initiative: Self-knowledge

Are you stressed out, overworked, feeling tired and out of control?

Then you could benefit from personal fitness training. More than two million people in the UK have engaged in some form of fitness training, and a growing number have their own personal fitness trainer. With busy, busy lives, many of us are too stressed, getting too little sleep, eating too much junk food and not doing enough exercise. You've heard it all before!

The good news is that growing numbers of people are deciding to act and do something for themselves. Lifestyle management starts by looking at how you live your life and deciding what you want to change. Making these changes is not easy, but the paybacks are considerable. Learning new habits of managing your personal fitness not only improves your physical appearance and well-being but also gives more energy, mental sharpness and general self-confidence.

Murray's story

With a big family reunion coming up in the summer, Murray wanted to get fitter and lose weight. With a demanding job and a growing family, Murray's life was full and he had no time to exercise. At 48, and not tall, he was 200 lb and

felt terrible. His parents had been overweight and his father had had diabetes. It was time to do something. But what? He had already tried dozens of different diets.

After talking with his GP, Murray contacted a personal fitness trainer and began to learn things about himself that he had not appreciated before. His trainer asked him to record his activities and consumption over seven days. This made grim reading. Although Murray thought of himself as eating a healthy diet, his trainer pointed out the lack of fruit and vegetables and the quantities of saturated fat and refined sugar. There were other surprises in this initial diagnosis. Murray knew that liquids were important but did not know that tea, coffee and even Coke were diuretics. 'Most of us are dehydrated for a lot of the time', his trainer said, 'you don't drink enough water.'

After various tests and analyses of Murray's current habits, the trainer helped him set some simple goals for the next ten weeks. They agreed on clear targets including a weight loss of 1 lb per week. Murray protested this at first because he wanted to lose more and faster. 'It's a trap to be too ambitious' insisted the trainer, 'be realistic and you will be able to sustain the effort and the improvement.' The trainer gave Murray diet sheets to follow and prescribed five exercise sessions per week of 30 minutes each.

After ten weeks, with twice-weekly sessions with his trainer, Murray had lost 11 lb and inches from his waist. His pulse was down, his metabolism was up and he generally felt better. From being only able to run a few steps, he could now run on a treadmill for 15 or even 20 minutes. There was some way to go to meet all his targets – and he had developed some new ones on the way – but he had made a good start.

Activity

This activity will help you diagnose and act on your personal fitness.

Step 1: Observation

Complete a seven-day log to get a picture of your lifestyle. It is important to collect data before deciding what to do. You can look at anything you want but some of the usual categories are suggested in the chart in Figure A38.1.

Step 2: Analysis

Looking at your seven-day log, what does it tell you about your lifestyle?
Compare it with the following general health advice.

	Mon	Tues	Wed	Thurs	Fri	Sat	Sun
Calorie intake – Breakfast – Lunch – Evening							
Portions fruit/veg.							
Caffeine intake							
Units of alcohol							
Cigarettes							
Stress level							
Exercise taken							

Figure A38.1 Lifestyle log

Diet

A woman with a sedentary job needs 1500–2000 calories per day, a man 2000–2500 (although these vary and depend on many factors, such as your metabolic rate).

■ *Breakfast* is the most important meal of the day – it wakes up your metabolism and powers your brain and body.
■ *Water* – drink lots of it – 2.5 litres per day at least – we are mainly composed of water and many common ailments stem from dehydration.

■ *Fruit and vegetables.* Try to eat at least five and up to ten 3-oz units of fruit and vegetables per day – cooked or raw, with as wide a range of colours as possible.

■ *Saturated fats.* Reduce these cholesterol-raising fats (mainly animal products – meat, cheese, full-fat milk) and increase *polyunsaturated* fats, which can lower blood cholesterol (mainly fruit and vegetables and oily fish – mackerel, salmon, etc.).

■ *Dietary fibre.* Soluble fibre as found in oats, peas, beans, fruit, etc., can also lower cholesterol in addition to scrubbing out your system.

■ *Variety* is an important word in diet – try writing down all the types of food you eat in a week. How many can you list? 10? 20? 30?

Around 30–50 types of food is a good target to give you all the vitamins and minerals you need. If you are below this, think about building in more variety, especially from fruit and vegetables where there is now a huge variety available.

Caffeine

One person who complained of dizziness and other symptoms logged her coffee intake and found it was over 20 cups per day. She worked in an office with a free vending machine. Try to limit your tea and coffee intake to 2–3 cups per day – drink water instead or decaffeinated coffee.

Alcohol

Government guidelines suggest a maximum of 2–3 units per day for women and 3–4 units for men. A unit is a half pint of ordinary beer or a small glass of wine or spirits. Try to have at least two alcohol-free days a week.

Cigarettes

You know the advice on this. Retirement annuities are much higher for smokers.

Stress

This is more difficult to diagnose on your own because it has many possible symptoms – a raised pulse, tiredness, irritability, inability to sleep, and so on. If you have noted any signs like these on your chart, then you should plan to reduce your stress levels. Common methods for this are exercise, yoga or meditation – but any way that you can relax and slow down – by reading, listening to music or doing the activities in this book – will help.

Exercise

The recommendation is for 30 minutes of moderate exercise five times per week. Moderate exercise is that which gets you slightly out of breath, slightly sweaty and warm. There are two basic types of exercise – resistance training and cardiovascular work. Resistance training involves building muscular tone, strength and endurance by exercising against some sort of resistance, for example using weights (e.g. hand-held weights, weights machines or your own body weight). Cardiovascular work or aerobic training (improving the efficiency of oxygen intake to your body) involves fast walking, jogging, running, cycling or swimming to raise the pulse and get your body working harder than normal.

The best form of exercise is the exercise that you enjoy taking.

N.B. If you have known health problems, or are seriously overweight, talk with your GP before undertaking any radical changes of diet or exercise. Radical lifestyle changes are not recommended in any case – slow and easy is the best way – but it might be a good idea to have a check-up anyway. Get clearance and encouragement to go ahead, and then you can go back to your doctor and show them later how well you have done.

Step 3: Setting goals and creating an action plan

Setting goals for health and lifestyle improvement is when personal trainers can be most helpful. The key thing is not to be too ambitious and avoid quick-fix diets and crash programmes of exercise.

To make your plan work, it has to fit with your current lifestyle. If you attend a lot of business dinners, what's your strategy for handling this aspect of your life? If you have small children or work long hours, how will you fit in five 30-minute slots of exercise?

Set some sensible longer-term targets and then set some goals for the next week (see Figure A38.2). Look for positive changes and set simple goals. If you had three glasses of wine last night, then have a night off tonight and buy yourself some delicious sparkling water!

Step 4: Reviewing progress

A weekly planner is good because it gives you a manageable target period for diet and exercise. At the end of each week, note any divergences from that week's plan and, before making your plan for the next week, decide if there are any modifications you need to make to hit your targets.

It nearly always helps if you have someone to discuss this with. Perhaps you can recruit your partner or someone at work to join you in this lifestyle management change?

Celebrate success when you hit your targets. Give yourself a treat that does not ruin your plan.

	Mon	Tues	Wed	Thurs	Fri	Sat	Sun
Calorie intake – Breakfast – Lunch – Evening							
Portions fruit/veg.							
Caffeine intake							
Units of alcohol							
Cigarettes							
Stress level							
Exercise taken							

Figure A38.2   Action plan

Follow-up

There are many sources of useful advice and help on personal fitness. Locally, you can talk to your GP – which you should certainly do if you have health problems or are very overweight. Other local professionals who can help include registered personal trainers and the staff at your local gymnasium or

sports centre. Here are some other places to start, including a free offer from the British Heart Foundation (BHF).

The British Heart Foundation has an informative website (www.bhf.org.uk/) and produces some useful materials including *So You Want to Lose Weight . . . for Good* and *Physical Activity for Weight Loss*, which are free booklets compiled by experienced nutritionists and available from the BHF at 14 Fitzhardinge Street, London W1H 4DH (020 7935 0185).

On general physical fitness we've already recommended *The Official British Army Fitness Guide* by Sam Murphy (Guardian Books, 2009) in Activity 34 and you might also find the Follow-ups to Activities 32 and 33 useful here. There are lots of other personal fitness books and DVDs, including Joanna Hall's *28 Day Total Body Plan* (2009).

The National Register of Premier Trainers and Therapists (www.nrpt.co.uk) at Parade House, 70 Fore Street, Trowbridge, Wiltshire BA14 8HQ (01225 253555) will tell you where to find a personal trainer or indeed how to become one.

Acknowledgement

This activity was created with the help of Sophie Barraclough, a Health and Wellbeing specialist, working from Holmfirth.

Who's the Boss?

Managerial qualities	**Initiative:** Analytical skills: People skills

In complex, interdependent social systems, decisions are rarely ours to take alone. Decisions about changes, decisions on problems, decisions about where to go and what to do are all made and often negotiated with those who are most concerned.

But who is really the 'boss' on the important decisions that affect your life? It should be you; and you should be able to choose the team to help you make good decisions and not hold you back. Some people will both give to and take from you; others will only take – their impact is largely destructive. The former cause you to grow and strengthen from your interaction with them; the latter weaken you.

This activity offers you an opportunity to select the team, and to be the boss, and even to remove those people whose influence is not helpful.

Activity

Step 1: The decision

Choose a decision you have to make in the near future. Don't choose a decision you have already made because the issue needs to be 'live'. The decision chosen should not be a simple choice between clear alternatives (e.g. choosing

a new car), but a complex matter involving others and their feelings and relationships, and affecting a number of areas of your life (e.g. making a decision
affecting your children, changing your job or some other aspect of your life).

Step 2: The board

Use the 'boardroom' diagram in Figure A39.1 to think about this decision. Write
in the names of the 'directors' who have a say in the making of this decision.
Choose the people in your life whom you trust or value to be your directors. Six
to twelve is a good number. Put their initials on the chairs around the table.

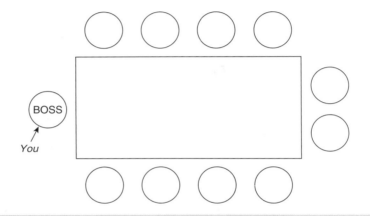

Figure A39.1   The boardroom

Step 3: The advice

Next to each of the 'directors' jot down notes on the advice that you think he
or she would give on this decision.

Step 4: Weighing the advice

Take a good look at this advice. Of each director in turn, ask yourself:

- Whose interest do they have at heart in making points, theirs or mine?
- Is she or he interested in getting a good decision or not?

Step 5: Confirming the team

As the boss, you take the decisions. You can also revise the management team,
although you can't remove people just because you don't like them. You need
to distinguish between liking a person and concern for a good decision. They
have a right to be there even if you don't like their advice.

Take a look at your management team:

(a) Are you really the boss?
(b) Are there any directors who shouldn't be there?
(c) Have you got enough advice of the right kind? Could you use a new director? Perhaps to replace one of your less useful directors?

Follow-up

This activity is putting you in charge of the important decisions in your life. If you and your boss sometimes seem to have difficulty in appreciating each other, try Activity 43, *Managing Upwards*, which makes a good follow-up. If you are in a hurry, you could turn to Sandi Mann's *Managing Your Boss in a Week* (Teach Yourself Books, 2012). A more collaborative approach can be found in Twyla Tharp's *The Collaborative Habit: Life Lessons for Working Together* (Simon & Schuster, 2010).

If you literally want to become your own boss, then from the same stable, Matt Avery's *Be Your Own Boss* (Teach Yourself Books, 2010) will help you to think about going it alone. On a broader front, Sara Williams' *The Financial Times Guide to Business Start Up 2013* (Pearson/FT Publishing, 2012) is an annually updated guide for entrepreneurs.

There are many websites to help in this area. The BBC website offers lots of resources at www.bbc.co.uk/news/business-16595152 and the HMRC (Her Majesty's Revenue and Customs) site is also very helpful: www.hmrc.gov.uk/startingup/index.htm.

Practising Change

Managerial qualities	**Initiative:** Sensitivity to events: Emotional resilience

Change is much talked about. In some organizations change has become an unquestioned necessity, an argument to influence people, even a fetish. It has become a treadmill that leads to the demand for yet more of it. And yet there are many questions about change: Does it always lead to better products or services? Are the changes made around here for the benefit of customers and users? Have previous changes been successful?

Yet, on the other hand, the complexities of life put a premium on personal and organizational flexibility. To get the best out of people, jobs, teams and organizations, we all need to become familiar with change processes and their effects. Leaders and managers do not just 'implement' changes (whatever their bosses may like to think); on many occasions they actively resist changes or seek to minimize their effects. To implement or resist, we need first to understand.

This activity includes experiments for learning about change and its effects. The aim is to practise change on yourself. What you learn as a result of the risks you take and the changes you experience will prepare you for those changes which are imposed on you and over which you have no control. It will also prepare you for planning change with other people – how it feels, what reactions to expect and how to cope with them.

Activities

Experiment 1: Eating a new food

The next time you go to a restaurant, or even the staff restaurant if the menu is varied enough, order a dish that you haven't tried before.

Before eating – note down

■ What are your expectations about the experience you are about to have?

_____

_____

_____

■ It is going to be pleasant or unpleasant, exciting or stressful?

_____

_____

_____

■ What are your feelings as you approach the food?

_____

_____

_____

While eating

■ Concentrate solely on eating, especially the first mouthful. Chew slowly, don't talk, and don't be distracted from the food.

After eating – note down

■ How does this compare with your normal approach to food?

_____

_____

_____

■ How much of a risk did you take?

_____

_____

_____

■ What did you gain as a result of your investment?

_____

_____

_____

■ What did you learn about changing to the unfamiliar?

_____

_____

_____

Experiment 2: Changing your surroundings

Choose a room where you spend considerable time. If you have an office, then this might be best, but any familiar room will do. This experiment involves rearranging the furniture, including taking down pictures, removing decorations or putting some new ones up.

Before rearranging – note down

■ Where else could the major pieces of furniture go?

_____

_____

_____

■ What other layout is possible?

_____

_____

_____

■   What alterations could be made to the decorations?

_____

_____

_____

Rearranging

■   Note carefully where you are putting things in your new arrangement.

After rearranging – note down

■   How comfortable do you feel now? (Allow at least a few hours before changing again.)

_____

_____

_____

■   What effect does the new layout have on you and your actions? What are you doing differently?

_____

_____

_____

■   How do other people react to your new layout? (Try and arrange for as many as possible to view and comment on the change.)

_____

_____

_____

■   What have you learned about the effects of physical surroundings?

_____

_____

_____

■   What have you learned about change and its effects on behaviour?

_____

_____

_____

If you learned something useful from this experiment, why not try another variation? How long is it since you looked at the fixtures and fittings of your managerial or leadership practice and considered a spring-clean or rearrangement?

Experiment 3: Changing your image

'Image management' is personal public relations. Try a few changes of image and wait for the results. For this experiment, take three aspects of yourself that have an obvious impact on the outside world, namely your styles of:

■   dress
■   writing
■   greeting.

Dress

Choose a simple change of dress. Leave your tie off or wear a hat. Put on a formal suit if you don't usually wear one; or try casual dress if you usually wear a suit. Embellish your appearance with accessories such as scarves, handkerchiefs, brooches.

As with all these experiments, take careful notes – before, during and after – of:

■   how you feel beforehand
■   how you feel during the introduction and implementation of the change
■   how other people react to you
■   what you learn about yourself and the effects of change.

Writing

Change your writing style – somehow. Are you a brief or lengthy writer? Are you conciliatory or aggressive in style? Serious or jokey?

Whatever you are or whatever your usual practice, try a change, e.g. write some humour into committee minutes.

Ask yourself the same questions as for 'Dress'.

Greeting

This is a surprisingly powerful communicator. First, you must recognize your usual routine. Do you greet everyone from cleaner to CEO with the same effusiveness or brevity? Do you sneak into work avoiding everyone's eyes?

Select a new approach and try it out. Give your friends a brief and business-like greeting and chat at length with the cleaners. Buttonhole the CEO in the lift and pass the time of day.

Ask yourself the same before, during and after questions.

For all these experiments, give yourself a few minutes of peace and reflection to extract the most from the experience.

Experiment 4: An unpleasant situation

This is the most difficult of the experiments and it is therefore recommended to graduates of the earlier ones.

Choose a situation that you know from experience you will probably not enjoy and would normally avoid.

This might be as simple as digging the garden or cleaning the lounge, or it might be more complex, like spending the whole evening on your own in a bar, or deliberately spending some time with a colleague whom you dislike.

Work through the following steps:

1. List some situations that you find unpleasant and try to avoid.

    _____

    _____

    _____

2. Pick one and deliberately put yourself into it.

    _____

    _____

    _____

3. Record your feelings on paper:

    ■ Before:

    _____

    _____

    _____

■ During:

_____

_____

_____

■ Afterwards:

_____

_____

_____

4. Write a short story changing the outcome of the experience.

_____

_____

_____

5. Identify how much personal responsibility you feel for what happened or did not happen.

_____

_____

_____

Follow-up

If you enjoyed these experiments and learned something about risk taking and the effects of change, generate some ideas for yourself about things you'd like to change – about yourself, about other people.

An early writer on such change was Albert Ellis, who said that there are four ways of handling an intolerable situation, namely change the situation, change your response to it, change yourself or leave the situation (see Activity 30, *Difficult Situations*). His *A Guide to Rational Living* (Wilshire Publications, 1975)

is still going strong after 25 years, but there are other more recent books on his Rational Emotive Therapy.

There are many books on so-called 'Change Management'. Mike Bourne's *Teach Yourself Change Management in a Week* (Teach Yourself Books, 2012) is simple but perhaps a little ambitious. The ubiquitous website www.business balls.com has interesting materials for personal change, including the Transition Curve and Personal Construct Psychology approaches: www. businessballs.com/personal-development.htm and www.businessballs.com/ leadership-management.htm.

Action Planning

Managerial qualities	**Initiative:** Analytical skills

Action planning is a key part of doing and learning. With small tasks it is semi-automatic – 'next time this happens, I'll do it this' – often without verbalizing or making it conscious. With bigger problems, automatic systems are rarely adequate. Sometimes, we jump into action before we have done sufficient thinking, and miss something important (although, as Activity 13, *Decision Making*, points out, sometimes action comes *before* planning).

An action plan involves setting targets for accomplishing an action. Part of this is establishing quality standards and also time deadlines. Once agreed or written down, your action plan becomes a commitment. Your action plan commits you to a course of action which you will achieve to a certain standard or by a certain date. It is this *commitment* that is one of the most important aspects of an action plan. Planning without commitment is a waste.

Activity

This activity follows an action planning sequence with a worked example. Choose your own issue to plan for and work it through in parallel. There are five stages:

1. setting goals
2. establishing sub-goals

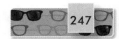

3. target dates
4. resources/methods
5. standards.

Or, if you prefer, you can use a short version, stages 1–3.

Step 1

Draw a chart upon which to detail your action plan. It should have five vertical columns (three if you are using the short method) and look something like Table A41.1.

Table A41.1   Action Plan Chart

Goals	Sub-goals	Target dates	Resources/ methods	Standards

Step 2

Choose a task or an issue that you want to act on or change. It does not have to be a big one. Choose something you are working on now or, perhaps, are about to start on.

If you are the sort of person who makes lists, you should have little difficulty in choosing a task – you will have a mental task list already. If you don't usually make lists, try doing one now.

For example, suppose you are asked to clear your desk in preparation for a top priority job coming in a month's time:

1. List all the things you would have to do in order to get your desk clear by then.

_____

_____

_____

2. Now choose the *most difficult* task on that list.

    Write your task in the left-hand column of the Action Plan Chart.

Step 3

Large tasks tend to look impossible, which gives us every opportunity to avoid them. Setting sub-goals breaks up the main task into manageable proportions. Questions that might throw up sub-goals include:

- What are the ways in which I could attain my goal?
- What is involved in this task?

The example worked through here is *Appraising the Work Team*:

- *Major goal*: Annual appraisals of the work team members
- *Sub-goals*:
    (a) Memo reminding all concerned of annual appraisal
    (b) Interviews with: Rose Smith; Maria Correlli; George Evans; Helga Martin; David Salmon
    (c) Complete paperwork and circulate for agreement
    (d) Make returns to Human Resources
    (e) Make individual action plans for any development needs arising.

Work your chosen goal into sub-goals and put them in the second column of the Action Plan Chart.

Step 4

Set target dates for your sub-goals first and then estimate the likely date for your overall goal. You may have a final deadline already, in which case you will have to work backwards to plan your sub-goal deadlines.

Fill in target completion dates on your Action Plan Chart. Remember these are your deadlines – failure to achieve them requires explanation – to yourself or to others.

If you're using the short Action Plan, you are now complete. Read the next two steps to see what isn't in your plan.

Step 5

The resources and methods column contains the answers to the questions:

- How am I going to tackle this problem?
- What alternative courses of action are open to me?
- What assistance do I need and what can I get?

In our example, resources include:

(a) Appropriate documentation from HR.
(b) HR notes on appraisal interviewing.
(c) Any other useful resources, e.g. training films, checklists, tips, etc.?
(d) Heather (source of advice).

Methods include:

(a) Circulating via intranet where appropriate and possible.
(b) Personal interviews.

In completing the resources and methods column, you may discover that you need to acquire more help before proceeding. If so, this becomes a sub-goal preceding the others.

Step 6

Now add some standards in the last column. These can be quantitative – clear measures that will demonstrate achievement of the goal or sub-goal; often they are qualitative measures that give you an idea or picture of when a task is completed satisfactorily.

By now you should have an Action Plan Chart, as in Table A41.2.

Step 7

Subject your Action Plan Chart to a critical appraisal. Perhaps you can ask someone who knows about you and the task to help. Examples of searching questions include:

- Is this goal really important for your department?
- Will these sub-goals lead to achievement of the main goal?
- Can that time target be shortened?
- Will those performance standards tell you how well you're doing?

Table A41.2 Completed Action Plan Chart

Goals	Sub-goals	Target dates	Resources/ methods	Standards
1. Appraising the work section		31 January		Sub-goal 2: 1. Develop personal, private and confidential climate
	1. Memo to all concerned	4 January	Resources: 1. Documentation (personnel)	2. End each interview only after:
	2. Interviews:			(a) got all information
	Rose Smith	18 January	2. Appraisal notes (last course)	(b) I feel I've improved relationship
	Maria Correlli	19 January		(c) Each interviewee has said
	George Evans	20 January	3. Anything else in personnel, films, etc.	all; been satisfied or agreed
	Helga Martin	21 January		a course of action
	David Salmon	22 January		
	3. Complete documentation and circulate		4. Jack Williamson	Sub-goal 3: Seek *commitment* rather than mere compliance
	4. Make returns to personnel	29 January		
			Methods:	Sub-goal 4: Ensure correctness to avoid return of documents
	5. Make individual action plans on any identified training needs	Say, by 1 March	1. Internal post 2. Personal interviews (90 minutes each)	
				Sub-goal 5: Action plans to conform with specification

An Action Plan Chart can give you a clear picture of what is involved in the completion of any complex task and help with the discipline and commitment necessary for its completion.

Follow-up

There are plentiful web-based materials on action planning. The Open University has a useful one at www.open.ac.uk/careers/produce-an-action-plan.php that breaks your career goals down into manageable steps. However, for those of you who never want to see an Action Plan ever again, you might like to try Action Learning – Reg Revans' proposal for helping people work with difficult issues in the company of like-minded colleagues – the *ABC of Action Learning* (Gower, 2011). In Action Learning you don't just plan, you *do*; and then reflect on what you've done in order to learn.

Imaging

When we 'image' something, we intend it to happen; that is the difference between *imaging* and *imagining*. A colleague used to 'think up a parking space' whenever he travelled to the head office building in town. On a particular day that I travelled with him, sure enough there was a vacant space when we got to the appointed spot. Coincidence? 'It's never failed yet,' he said, matter-of-factly.

The idea of bringing about reality through thought has been around a long time. Prayer is perhaps the most common form of this. The power of positive thinking is used by high-performing people in many fields of endeavour to visualize the results they want. In work organizations, it is normal to talk about leaders or managers with (or without) *vision*. This is the recognition that for things to happen, we must first create a picture of what we want to happen. 'What will it look like?' comes even before 'What's in it for me?'

Imaging is the everyday activity of creating a vivid picture of what we want to bring about – at work, in relationships and in ourselves.

Activity

Step 1

Choose a situation, a relationship or an aspect of yourself that you would like to change or influence. You could choose something that came up in the career planning activity (Chapter 3).

Step 2

Think about this aspect of work, relationship or yourself. Try to build up a picture of how you would like it to look:

■ What would be the best picture you could imagine?

_____

_____

_____

■ Now what do you want it to look like?

_____

_____

_____

Visualize the results you want in this situation.

You might find this difficult to visualize. Some people can picture things easily, but others don't. If you are having difficulty, try writing or drawing to help with your imaging:

1. Write down a list of what you'd like to see in that situation, e.g.
   ■ 'I want my relationship with Alice to be more friendly; less "careful".'
   ■ 'I want to see us finish the Anshan project on time. I see the team celebrating our success in the Victoria.'
   ■ 'I see myself volunteering to lead the same team on a new project.'
   ■ Etc.

Re-visit this list at least once a day for a week – adding to it and embellishing it.

2. Draw a picture (or, for non-drawers, make a collage by cutting and pasting pictures and images from magazines) of the image of what you want. When you have a picture, re-visit it at least once a day for a week – adding to it and embellishing it. For example, if I want to change my room, I can cut out from this magazine just the sort of desk I want; I can photograph or draw what I want to keep from my existing things. I can try out all sorts of decors, furniture, plants, equipment, on paper. I can experiment with layout and even ask other people what they think before taking the plunge.

Step 3

When you have a good picture of what you want to bring about, keep thinking about it, bringing it back to mind or taking it out to focus on it from time to time.

Over time, and without planning in detail, your image of what you want will begin to appear through the working of your intuition in the multitude of everyday decisions.

Step 4

For those who lack confidence or who perhaps are put off by the idea of 'tempting fate', it is really just a creative alternative to the managerial stock in trade of planning, i.e. attempting to influence future events. 'Imaging' is perhaps a necessary precursor to planning; it can add some magic to the managerial culture, with all its graphs, printouts and flow charts.

Maintaining an image requires strength and stamina. All too often the vision fades and the magic is lost. One way to sustain yourself is by daily *affirmation*. This is simply saying to yourself (or writing down) a positive statement about yourself and your image. For example, if I was determined to become less irritable and I had an image of myself as smiling and relaxed, I might say, 'I, Mike, am becoming more relaxed and smiling every day.' If you were imaging a more creative, productive team, you could say, 'Every day, in every way, this team is getting more creative and more productive.'

Try a suitable positive affirmation, naming yourself or the people or the situation and say it to yourself every day, perhaps out loud, preferably several times, say, six. Alternatively, or additionally, you can write down your affirmation. Do this 20 times each day.

If you feel a bit silly 'affirming yourself', think about this: perhaps being able to be silly at times is an important aspect of creativity and of having fun – 'I didn't get where I am today without . . . !'

Having fun is one aspect of 'imaging', but the power in this is not to be taken lightly. Use 'imaging' for good ends, not to denigrate people – and constantly question your definition of 'good' in this situation.

Follow-up

From the bookshop's self-development shelves Shakti Gawain's *Creative Visualization* (New World Library, 2002) is a guide to visualization and achieving the things you want. Chris Bilton's *Management and Creativity: From Creative Industries to Creative Management* (Wiley, 2006) takes a very different view, exploring the relationship between the management of creativity and creative approaches to management.

Managing Upwards

Managerial qualities	**Initiative:** People skills

Is your working life being ruined by your relationship with your boss?

One of the most persistent complaints of young managers in organizations is about the quality of their bosses. A recent group of senior professionals in a large utility came up with the following grumbles: My boss . . .

- is always too busy
- thinks that things manage themselves
- doesn't listen to me
- never gives me feedback
- only criticizes, never praises
- gives me ridiculous deadlines
- has very obvious favourites
- picks on me and finds fault with my work
- is anxious for me not 'to rock the boat'
- wants to pass off any good ideas as their own
- spends most of their time looking upwards and trying to please their boss
- fails to get a fair share of resources for our department

and, most of all . . .

- is not interested in my learning and development.

For professionals and 'knowledge workers', the preferred boss is a senior colleague rather than a supervisor, a mentor rather than an overseer, more of an adviser and consultant than a work allocator and quality controller.

If your boss hasn't got these messages yet – how can you help him or her to work more in this way? And help yourself in the process?

Rosie's tale (Part 1)

Rosie was a graduate engineer just two years out of university and working on what should have been an exciting marine propulsion technology project. But her boss cast a cloud over her working life, and indeed her life in general.

'Even now, three years on, it makes my blood run cold to think about him,' she says, 'work could have been so different, if he had been a better manager.' Tony (her current boss) is such a contrast – he sees his job as enabling his staff to get on with their work and helping them sort out the tasks. He handles all the politics for the department and generally tries to make life easier for staff. 'It was unfortunate for me that Derrick was my first experience of having a manager – if it happened to me now I would know what to do – but then I just put up with it.'

Derrick did not see himself as a manager at all, he saw himself as a technical specialist. He would say things like, 'I'm very lucky because you all get on with what you have to do and I don't have to manage you', but at the same time he would say, 'I can't understand why all my staff leave so quickly.' The answer to that was because his staff got so fed up with his complete inability to plan or prioritize work, or to give notice of critical jobs. 'He would suddenly drop jobs on you that had been on his desk for days and tell you that it was needed tomorrow. Then he wouldn't give you any feedback and you would never really know whether the customer – usually another department – was pleased with the work or not. Naturally, people used to leave as soon as they had the opportunity. Tony's staff leave too but that is because he encourages us to move on to bigger things and really makes sure that we get developed while we're here – it's just totally different.'

'Another thing about Derrick was that he was really naive about politics. He was intransigent and would refuse to compromise. It got us – the department – a bad name in the company. The rest of the organization tends to write you off if you don't deliver, and this is disastrous for our careers as well as for the department.'

Rosie was infuriated, but she also felt sorry for Derrick; as a manager, he was a duck out of water and his home life didn't sound too good either. Something had to be done.

Activity

If you spend time grumbling about your boss, or you feel that their actions are affecting your effectiveness, perhaps it is time for you to do something about it? This activity will help you to come up with some ideas for action to manage your boss better. You can then go on to read Part 2 of Rosie's Tale to see what she did next.

Step 1: Analysis

Take a close look at your relationship with your boss.

1. First, make a list of all those things that you consider to be good about it, and those that are bad. Consider such things as:

   - work allocation
   - time for consultations and discussions
   - listening
   - willingness to share knowledge
   - feedback on work done
   - information about the organization
   - help with tasks
   - access to knowledge
   - variety of work and access to special projects
   - attention paid to personal development and learning
   - career development.

   Are there any other important aspects to your relationship that you can think of?

2. Second, make a list of those things which you would like your boss to . . .

   - Stop doing

   _____

   _____

   _____

   - Start doing

   _____

   _____

   _____

■ Continue to do

_____

_____

_____

These three lists are critical and should give you the basis for a conversation with your boss. However, until now this exercise has been risk-free; Step 2 is more testing.

Step 2: Make an appointment

Ask your boss for a private one-hour meeting to discuss your work. It will be helpful to let them have some idea of what you have in mind.

If you have a good relationship with your boss, you could just suggest that they also prepare for the meeting by competing the three lists above about you. You can then work from the lists at the meeting.

If your relationship is less secure, you could say something like:

I have been thinking about my job performance and have come up with some ideas to improve my effectiveness. As you could help me with some of these things, I'd like the opportunity of talking with you at some length about them.

Step 3: Negotiation meeting

Whichever way you do it, this is essentially a negotiation. So you should prepare for the meeting as you would for any negotiation:

1. What are your key goals? What do you want to achieve?

_____

_____

_____

2. What do you have to offer the other person? What's in it for them?

_____

_____

_____

3. What is your bottom line for an agreement? What is your 'fall back' – the least you will settle for?

_____

_____

_____

Always have a fall-back goal in mind in case the meeting does not go as planned. This might even be just to get agreement to a further meeting after you have both had a chance to reflect.

Step 4: Agreement and review

All good negotiations end with an agreement – and it is usually worth putting it in writing. Tell your boss you will write up the agreed points and send them a copy.

Also, agree a review date to discuss progress after a month or two and put this in your diaries.

If you can manage this, you will become more confident in dealings with your boss. Confidence begets confidence and Step 2, fixing that appointment, may be the critical point in a journey to a better working life for both of you.

So, what did Rosie do next?

Rosie's tale (Part 2)

Rosie got a clue to the way forward one day when she lost her temper. She was handling some requests on expenditure targets but when she took them in to Derrick, he was busy and said, 'Stuff them, I'm not doing that.' Rosie knew that Finance's cooperation was essential to the progress of several of their key projects, and she got mad and put her foot down, insisting that they put the figures in. She did most of the work and made sure they were sent off. Rosie told this story to her four immediate professional colleagues and they decided to act together to improve the things they were grumbling about.

The first thing was the team meetings. They weren't proper meetings, but rambling sessions with Derrick from time to time. The team called the next meeting and set an agenda of critical items demanding action which they divided up and prepared in advance. It was immediately obvious that by talking tasks through, people began to understand what each of them was doing and working on. Derrick didn't seem to mind at all – he hated meetings

anyway – 'You've said more useful things at this meeting than I've heard in the last year,' he said.

As the meetings continued with team members taking the chair in turn, the benefits of understanding the whole work of the department began to pay off, with a much better sense of joint priorities and targets. Derrick's job was to present each meeting with any new tasks well in advance of their deadlines. After six months of this collective effort, the external perceptions of the department also improved greatly. It was suddenly obvious how much was getting done – and how limited the departmental influence had been before. Derrick was no different but at least one thing in his life had improved.

Follow-up

There is a rich vein of books on this theme, many of which take the view that your boss is basically the problem. The classic *Managing Your Boss* (*Harvard Business Review*, January/February 1980, pp. 92–100), by John Gabarro and John Kotter, is still worth a visit. Perhaps the best title on this issue is Bob Weinstein's *I Hate My Boss!: How to Survive and Get Ahead when Your Boss is a Tyrant, Control Freak or Just Plain Nuts* (McGraw-Hill, 1998), which includes all sorts of interesting and amusing strategies.

Mike Leibling's *How People Tick: A Guide to Over 50 Types of Difficult People and How to Handle Them* (Kogan Page, 2009) broadens the approach to include all the sorts of people that we experience as difficult.

Beyond 'Yes ... But ...'

Managerial qualities	**Creativity:** Analytical skills: Self-knowledge

Are you familiar with that bad feeling of putting forward new ideas – to the boss or to other authorities – only to find them blocked or rejected without a fair hearing?

How often is the boot on the other foot? How often do you say, 'Yes ... but ...' and reject ideas without a fair hearing? It probably happens more than you think, because accepting other people's ideas is difficult.

Activity

Look out for occasions on which you may reject other people's ideas: at meetings, in projects, as part of your day-to-day work with others ...

Step 1

When you recognize such an occasion, get a pad and pen and write down as many possible reasons as you can think of as to why you reject an idea.

Write them down without qualification, evaluation or discussion. *Be open and honest.* Such a list could include:

- ■ The idea is impractical.
- ■ It's too expensive.

- ▇ It's administratively inconvenient.
- ▇ It challenges my basic beliefs.
- ▇ It will cause a lot of political headaches.
- ▇ It involves risks that I am not prepared to take.
- ▇ It makes me feel unnecessary, redundant.
- ▇ It devalues my ideas or role.
- ▇ I just don't like/respect the person putting forward the idea.
- ▇ I find it hard to accept that other people in general, or this person in particular, can have better ideas than me.
- ▇ It will cause me to lose face, to backtrack on previously stated ideas or beliefs.
- ▇ I don't want this other person to take the credit.

Step 2

Look over the reasons you have given. Challenge them. Cross-examine yourself. Imagine you are a barrister challenging a witness (yourself). For example:

- ▇ How do you know it's impracticable? Have you tried it? What happened? Why? Why not?
- ▇ What do you mean, too expensive? What are the detailed costs and benefits? How could it be done cheaper? It's your job to be able to do this, isn't it?
- ▇ Are you sure you are not rejecting this idea because of the person who made it? What would you say if I pointed out that you nearly always reject ideas put forward by this person? Why is this?

And so on.

This technique of self-cross-examination is very powerful (it is a particular version of Activity 56, *Conversations with Yourself*).

Step 3

What you do next depends on your 'verdict' following self-examination.

Having identified some of the *real* reasons why you are blocking/rejecting an idea, you will need to explore these further – with yourself and with the other people concerned.

Draw up a list of changes that you will make in response to an idea ('I will try, with the others concerned, to *make* the thing practicable, to *cut* its costs, to *overcome* administrative/political difficulties').

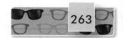

Step 4: Active listening

Whatever else you do from now on, practise *active listening* whenever someone is presenting an idea.

Passive listening is paying just enough attention to note matters of interest; *active listening* is making a conscious attempt to work out what the other person is trying to say, expressing your attention and interest, verbally and non-verbally, and generally encouraging the other in getting their ideas across.

Follow-up

Wikipedia has a useful page on Active Listening (en.wikipedia.org/wiki/Active_listening) and you can find tools for learning how to listen better at www.mindtools.com/public_search.php?format2=builtin-lang&sport2=score&method2=and&words=communication+skills.

Generating New Ideas

Managerial qualities	**Creativity:** Analytical skills

Nothing blocks creativity like premature judgement. New solutions and ideas are by definition unusual, so we reject them as nonsensical, impracticable, expensive, unrealistic – the 'Yes . . . But . . .' syndrome. See Activity 44.

Stereotyping or narrow vision is another common blocker. Used to doing things in certain ways, we close our minds to alternatives, so that after a time they just never occur to us.

Here is a technique designed to generate new ideas and to overcome the blocks to creative thinking. It can be done individually or in a group.

Activity

To get a sense of the idea-generating process, here is a simple example.

Step 1

Write down the answer to the following question:

'What are paper clips used for?'

_____

_____

_____

Unless you are a relatively fluent and innovative thinker, you may only have generated one or two uses for paper clips. For example, you may have said something about 'holding two or more pieces of paper together'.

Step 2

Now write down, in five minutes, as many *other possible* uses of paper clips as you can think of.

Don't worry how unusual, peculiar or odd some of these might be. Write them down and keep thinking of more until the five minutes is up.

_____

_____

_____

_____

_____

Step 3

Individual lists will be very different. Groups can usually generate far more ideas in five minutes. You may have come up with between 10 and 30 possible uses. Here is a partial list grouped by some of the attributes of paper clips – you will be able to add to this:

- hooks: paper hooks; use for unlocking doors
- links: chains
- pins: cocktail sticks, notice pins
- connectors: fuse, contact maker
- bindings: wire, staple
- centres: axles, spindles, spigots
- magnets: picking up light ferrous objects from narrow or bent holes

■ piercing tool: punching small holes, stitches, belt holes
■ weapon: use defensively to stab.

The more attributes you see and make use of, the more you overcome the stereotyping problem.

Making the list quickly and forcing the pace helps to overcome the premature evaluation blockage. There just isn't the time for the 'Yes … Buts …'.

Step 4

Now think of a real problem facing you.

Again, without pausing for evaluation, force yourself to list as many possible solutions as you can.

Don't at this stage allow yourself to consider all the implications, pros and cons of each solution. Just get a good list – the longer the better.

_____

_____

_____

_____

_____

Groups are often very effective in generating new ideas. State the problem and have members compete in shouting out possible solutions, which are written up on a flip chart. During this process, it is vital that no evaluation takes place. It is only when ideas are exhausted, and a very full list has been prepared, that careful, considered evaluation should be attempted.

Step 5

Now is the time to evaluate these possible solutions.

Take each in turn, try to remain open-minded about them, consider all their strengths, weaknesses, consequences, requirements and implications.

Follow-up

You will find Activity 16, _Planning Change_, and Activity 41, _Action Planning_, useful in generating good new ideas.

Twyla Tharp's *The Creative Habit: Learn It and Use It for Life* (Simon & Schuster, 2007) takes an artistic stance to management and leadership, while supermarket founder Ken Robinson's *Out of Our Minds: Learning to Be Creative* (Capstone, 2nd edition, 2011) is a businessman's plea for greater creativity in education and business.

Once again, MindTools (www.mindtools.com/pages/main/newMN_CT.htm) offers starters on a wide range of techniques to help you generate *creative* solutions to your problems.

Approaches to Creativity

Managerial qualities	**Creativity**

There are many techniques and approaches to creative problem solving. Here are a few of them:

- *Draw the problem*:
  Whether or not it is a visual or spatial problem, represent it somehow as a picture or cartoon. Be as uninhibited as you can.

  Now, consider possible solutions to the problem, and draw them.

- *Be the problem, or part of it*:
  Imagine that you are the troublesome part of the machine, or the lost or broken object, or the misunderstood message. Think hard about how you feel. What could be done? What would help?

- *Imagine something completely different*:
  Think of, imagine, anything – an object, an event, an idea; for instance, a spider's web, or a football match, or dissolving.

  Concentrate on this image in relation to the problem at hand. What's the link? Can you get a fresh perspective to help solve the problem?

- *Invert the problem*:
  Turn the problem inside out or upside down, or reverse it.

  For example, instead of putting a product into a package, consider putting a package round a product; instead of protecting employees from an industrial accident, protect the accident from the staff.

■ *Turn the problem into an opportunity:*
As the ancient saying has it, 'every problem is an opportunity'. For whom is this a problem? For whom is it an opportunity? Where is the opportunity in this?

■ *Write a story:*
Fictionalize the problem and the people concerned with it. How did it happen? Who does what next? How does it end? You could get a completely new angle on the situation.

Activity

Now choose one or more of the real problems from your work situation. Try each of the approaches on it:

■ Draw it.
■ Be the problem.
■ Imagine something completely different.
■ Invert the problem.
■ Think of the opportunities that could arise from the problem.
■ Write the story.

Note down all ideas and possible solutions – however fanciful.

In the light of the ideas you generate, reflect on which of the approaches helped you the most.

Follow-up

To become truly creative, you must let yourself go a little. Try some of the other activities for developing creativity in this book and have a go.

The books listed under the previous activity will also be useful here. For an alternative approach, Andrew Robinson's *Genius: A Very Short Introduction* (Oxford University Press, 2011) uses the life and work of familiar geniuses to highlight the various factors such as talent, heredity, parenting, education, training, hard work and luck that contribute to the making of genius.

Wikipedia has a through treatment of creativity, listing several schools and approaches and linking it with intelligence and other psychological concepts: http://en.wikipedia.org/wiki/Creativity.

Attribute Alternatives

Managerial qualities	**Creativity**

We often get stuck in routine ways of doing things and locked in by our assumptions about the way things should be done.

A way to overcome these constraints is to identify the attributes of the current method and then generate a list of alternative attributes.

Activity

Step 1

Choose a current task that you suspect might be done differently or better. Note down the method or device currently in use, with its main characteristics and attributes.

In the newspaper industry, for example, take the threat to the conventional newspaper in the digital age. Current medium – broadsheet or tabloid conventional paper.

Step 2

Take each of the attributes and consider alternatives to it. You could use the approach in Activity 45, *Generating New Ideas*, here.

List any alternatives that come to mind and do not attempt to evaluate them. No matter how silly or impractical it seems, list it. With the example above, the following alternatives are possible:

- Made of: (paper) reprintable medium, reprogrammable special item, CD, downloadable.
- Life: (disposable) returnable, refreshable, reprogrammable.
- Delivery: (shop or home delivery) phone, e-mail, 'cash point' style update of paper, mobile phone access, etc.
- Frequency: (daily/weekly) frequently, continuously, on access.

Step 3

Examine and evaluate the alternatives. Consider possible combinations. From the hundreds of potential permutations, choose some of the more likely combinations.

Examine these for practicability. The ideas might be logically or technically feasible, but have to be, and many people may still be uncomfortable with high-tech delivery processes. We may value, for example, conventional papers for other purposes – lighting fires, wrapping things, etc.

Follow-up

Keep trying this exercise with real problems. Remember the important rule: generate as many alternatives as possible, but leave evaluation until later.

For further ideas, you will find the sources listed under Activity 45, *Generating New Ideas*, and Activity 46, *Approaches to Creativity*, of value.

Your Multiple Intelligences

Managerial qualities	**Mental agility:** Creativity: Self-knowledge

Howard Gardner's theory of multiple intelligences suggests that human beings possess many kinds of intelligence. He questions the idea of the single measure of general intelligence as simply measured by IQ tests:

> In the heyday of the psychometric and behaviorist eras, it was generally believed that intelligence was a single entity that was inherited; and that human beings – initially a blank slate – could be trained to learn anything, provided that it was presented in an appropriate way. Nowadays an increasing number of researchers believe precisely the opposite; that there exists a multitude of intelligences, quite independent of each other; that each intelligence has its own strengths and constraints; that the mind is far from unencumbered at birth; and that it is unexpectedly difficult to teach things that go against early 'naive' theories that challenge the natural lines of force within an intelligence and its matching domains.

(H. Gardner, 1993, p. xxiii)

Although Gardner's theory has been criticized, it accords with much common-sense experience: we do think and learn in many different ways. There are eight types of intelligence in this theory:

- bodily/physical/kinaesthetic
- linguistic

- mathematical-logical
- visual/spatial
- musical
- interpersonal
- intrapersonal
- naturalist.

There are also various other possibilities being considered, including spiritual, moral and existential intelligences.

Here is a questionnaire for you to assess your own multiple intelligences.

Activity

Step 1: Multiple intelligences questionnaire

Complete the questionnaire in Table A48.1, scoring 1–5 for each item depending upon how true this is of you.

Table A48.1 **Multiple intelligences questionnaire**

Item no.	Item	Score 1 – not true of me 2 – slightly true of me 3 – quite a bit true of me 4 – definitely true of me 5 – very true of me
1	I like to deal with problems physically, to get directly involved, get 'hands on'	
2	I appreciate books, radio, plays, poetry, playing with words	
3	I like to solve puzzles and problems	
4	I have a good sense of direction – where I am, which way I need to go	
5	I enjoy music – listening or playing	
6	I am interested in how other people think and feel	
7	I like to reflect on things that have happened and what I can learn from them	
8	I remember things about animals, birds, plants, and so on	
9	I am skilful when working with things	

(continued)

Table A48.1 *(continued)*

Item no.	Item	Score 1 – not true of me 2 – slightly true of me 3 – quite a bit true of me 4 – definitely true of me 5 – very true of me
10	I learn well from books, lectures or tapes	
11	I like logical explanations	
12	I am observant, I notice what others do not	
13	I have a good sense of rhythm and/or melody	
14	I am sensitive to other people's moods and reactions	
15	I enjoy doing things independently of others	
16	I notice things in the environment that others often miss	
17	I enjoy physical activity – walking, dancing, games, swimming, etc.	
18	I talk well and have a large vocabulary	
19	I like to arrange tasks in a neat and orderly sequences	
20	I can see things clearly in 'my mind's eye' (e.g. a familiar room)	
21	I find it easy to learn songs and lyrics	
22	I can help with difficulties between people	
23	I appreciate privacy and quiet for working and thinking	
24	I am concerned about the environment and endangered species	
25	I like to be moving, doing and touching things that I am learning about	
26	I am good at explaining things	
27	I look for patterns and relationships between things	
28	I find that films, slides, videos, pictures help me to learn	
29	I enjoy listening to sounds in nature	
30	I get involved in clubs, groups and social activities	
31	I reflect on my own feelings and thoughts and why I do things	
32	My sensory skills of sight, sound, taste, smell, touch are keen	
33	I remember best what I have done – compared with what I have seen or heard	

Item no.	Item	Score 1 – not true of me 2 – slightly true of me 3 – quite a bit true of me 4 – definitely true of me 5 – very true of me
34	I like to write things down, take notes	
35	I approach tasks/problems in a logical, step-by-step way	
36	I like to use charts, diagrams, mind maps, pictures to help me to learn	
37	I can easily remember tunes	
38	I enjoy discussing things and ideas with others	
39	I like to think about the purpose of what I am doing and learning	
40	I easily learn characteristics, names, categorizations and data about objects or species found in the natural world	

Step 2: Scoring

Now score the questionnaire in Table A48.2, adding up the numbers for each of the items listed against each of the multiple intelligence categories.

The maximum score is 25 and the minimum is 5.

Table A48.2 Multiple intelligences scoring key

'Intelligence'	Item numbers	Total score
Bodily/physical/kinaesthetic	1, 9, 17, 25, 33	
Linguistic	2, 10, 18, 26, 34	
Mathematical-logical	3, 11, 19, 27, 35	
Visual/spatial	4, 12, 20, 28, 36	
Musical	5, 13, 21, 29, 37	
Interpersonal	6, 14, 22, 30, 38	
Intrapersonal	7, 15, 23, 31, 39	
Naturalist	8, 16, 24, 32, 40	

Step 3: So what?

Now map your eight intelligence scores on to the 'spider's web' in Figure A48.1.

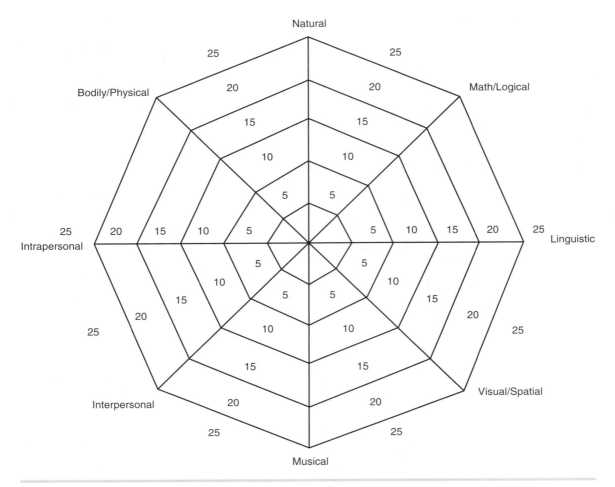

Figure A48.1   Gardner's eight intelligences profile

The 'spider's web' enables you to draw up a profile of your scores on each of the eight intelligences. What does your profile mean? Here are a few possibilities to get you thinking:

■ If you scored between 20 and 25 in any one dimension, then you are high in this form of intelligence; if you scored from 5 to 10, then this is an underdeveloped area for you.

■ The profile can indicate your current preferences, and also those areas of experience that you currently avoid. One way to work with this is deliberately to try to use your less favoured intelligences; for example, if you are high on intrapersonal, but low on interpersonal, then make yourself go

and talk with other people about issues that you would normally keep to yourself.

■ Conversely, if you are very high on interpersonal, but low on intrapersonal, then take time out alone to reflect on what something might be telling you, what it means for you. How do you personally think and feel about it?

■ If you are low on spatial intelligence, draw a picture of a situation that you find yourself in at work or at home.

■ Another possibility is that you might find that you are high on an intelligence that you don't get an opportunity to use at work. In this case, what sort of work would enable you to exploit your talent? Who, in your organization, uses this sort of ability? Go and talk to them, exploring how you could do more with what you've got.

These are only a few of the possibilities arising from assessing your multiple intelligences. To take this further, you probably need to read more about the idea and consult with other people about what this might mean for you.

Follow-up

Howard Gardner has supplemented his classic text *Frames of Mind: The Theory of Multiple Intelligences* (Basic Books, 1993) with a useful review of the issues, additions and criticisms raised by his theory: *Intelligence Reframed: Multiple Intelligences for the 21st Century* (Basic Books, 2000).

As ever, there is a great deal on the web. Enter 'multiple intelligences' and this will provide you with more than you can deal with. You could start with *infed*, which is an independent not-for-profit site put together by a small group of educators: www.infed.org/thinkers/gardner.htm.

Coping with Complexity

Managerial qualities	**Mental agility:** Emotional resilience

Too much change in too short a time can result in stress and disorientation in rats and humans.

Coping with and adapting to change call for great effort in terms of emotional stability and of learning new skills and new knowledge.

Mental agility or 'flexible intelligence' is an ability – potential or realized – that all of us have to some extent. Unlike the old-fashioned and fixed view of 'intelligence' as being associated with crude tests of 'general intelligence' or 'IQ', mental agility can be improved with practice like any other skill.

Mental agility is the ability that allows us to do several things at once, switching our minds and resources from one topic to another, making hundreds of decisions as we do so, storing information, recalling it – in short, what we all do in a multi-task situations.

Consider the mental agility requirements of the parent's job, e.g.:

Prepare breakfast for four people *simultaneously with*:

- finding and putting together two lots of dinner money
- cleaning two pairs of shoes
- listening to the news on the radio
- brushing two lots of hair
- talking lovingly to partner
- talking lovingly to children
- dealing with sundry contingencies – all in 30 minutes.

How did you get on?

There are many forms of complex work, which we learn and then do instinctively. The teacher in a classroom, the retail supervisor, the team manager, all pursue multiple tasks, observe thousands of stimuli, attend to a few, make appropriate multiple responses and so on. And all without much conscious thought about the complexity of the situation. We don't usually reflect on our complex skills and how this learning may be applied as a general skill to new situations.

Activity

This activity invites you to work on certain multiple tasks and consciously reflect about how you are adapting to the skill requirements of doing several simultaneous tasks.

Step 1

Find a free hour for this activity (a tough task in itself). Now choose six tasks, suitable for your particular circumstances. For example, if you are at work, these could include:

- writing a paper or notes for a meeting
- planning your key outputs for the next six months
- catching up with your e-mails
- telephoning three or four people you need to contact
- talking to a colleague about something which interests them
- preparing statistics
- filling in government forms (an Inland Revenue form is ideal)
- planning the best new arrangement for your workspace
- reading a management book
- doing *The Times* crossword.

Step 2

Estimate how long each task will take; add up the total time and halve it (you only ever have half the time you need).

Now, try to complete all the tasks in that time. Don't do them sequentially, do them all at once, switching from one to another.

N.B. If you find switching from one task to another hard, then do it mechanically. Number the tasks 1 to 6; divide your allotted time and, using a dice, change tasks after every 3 or 5 minutes. This will be difficult at first, but your flexibility will improve.

Step 3

Now reflect on your experience. Note down your responses to the following questions:

1. How did I do in terms of completing the tasks?

    _____

    _____

    _____

2. What feelings did I have during this experiment? (Record all the phrases/ adjectives that spring to mind.)

    _____

    _____

    _____

3. Have I ever felt like this before? When? What was the outcome then?

    _____

    _____

    _____

4. Could I have been better organized or better prepared? How would I do it better next time?

    _____

    _____

    _____

5. How can I increase my general ability to deal with multi-task situations?

    _____

    _____

    _____

To exercise and increase your mental agility, repeat this experiment in other situations. The important thing is to be aware of what you are doing and when you are doing it.

Always make time for reflection afterwards. Without this you may miss the learning potential of your own experiences.

Follow-up

Complexity is a topic in itself. For a simple introduction to complexity theory, look at Melanie Mitchell's *Complexity: A Guided Tour* (Oxford University Press, 2011), which is an award-winning review of the concept as applied to biological, technological and social matters.

Ralph Stacey applies these ideas to management and organizations in *Complexity and Organizational Reality: Uncertainty and the Need to Rethink Management after the Collapse of Investment Capitalism* (Routledge, 2009). There is a school of thinking about leadership derived from complexity theory which you can explore at:

complexityleadership.wikispaces.com/Overview+of+Theories.

Just a Minute

Managerial qualities	**Mental agility:** People skills

Leadership and managerial work often demand an ability to think through complex matters, to think quickly on one's feet and to switch rapidly from one problem to another.

There is a widely held belief that intelligence is innate and cannot be developed through training. This idea comes from early psychological theories that have long since been questioned and rejected. Current thinking suggests that the kind of mental abilities that make up intelligence can improve significantly through experience and practice. The following activity is designed to give you practice in thinking quickly on your feet.

Activity

You need ten filing cards or small pieces of paper, and a digital recorder.

Step 1

Write one of the following topics on each of five cards:

- home working
- self-managed team working
- e-commerce

- workaholism
- safety.

Step 2

On each of the remaining five cards, write one of the following audiences:

- group of government inspectors
- party of visiting Korean business people
- visiting party of final-year university undergraduates
- party of South American tourists
- group of senior citizens.

Shuffle the two sets of cards separately and put the two piles face down.

Step 3

Turn on the recorder. Pick up the first card on each pile and talk for one minute on the revealed topic, to the indicated audience. After a minute, pick up the second topic and audience cards and talk for another minute. Repeat this until you have used all the cards.

Play back the tape to review how well you did in keeping to the topic and relating it to the audience in each instance.

Obviously, if you wish, choose your own topics and audiences to suit your situation better.

Follow-up

Thinking skills come with practice, so the more you can exercise them, the more they will develop.

You should be able to find plenty of opportunities for this in the context of your work. If you want to test yourself on IQ-type tests, there are many of these on the web. Management and business bookshops also sell practice versions of the *Princeton Test* – the one most often used for selection to Business School MBA programmes. *The IQ and Psychometric Test Workbook*, by Philip Carter (Kogan Page, 2011), is a self-test workbook.

A Helicopter Mind

An extensive study of managers concluded that the 'helicopter mind' is a key determinant of success. This is the ability to think in both concrete and abstract terms, and to move rapidly between the two, linking abstract ideas to specific actions and vice versa. Leaders and managers who think in this way are good at linking theory to practice so that each improves the other.

Whether thinking moves 'up' to the abstract or 'down' to the specific depends on the questions asked: 'Why?' questions move you up, 'How?' questions move you down.

For example, the task of selecting people can be analysed in the following way:

WHY? – To produce enough to meet orders

WHY? – To get good enough people to work the machines

TASK – SELECT PEOPLE FOR JOBS

HOW? – Assess skills needed, test applicants for these

HOW? – Study existing staff, develop tests to demonstrate skills

If you start with a statement of fact, you can ask: WHY is this true? And HOW can this be applied? See, for example, Figure A51.1.

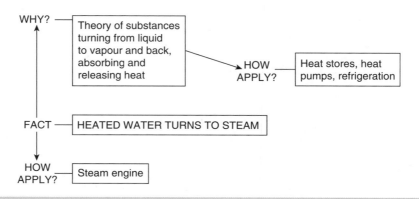

Figure A51.1   'How' and 'why' thinking

Once the 'Why?' questions are answered, moving down again with 'How?' questions can help generate new alternatives and ideas. In the example above, the answer to the 'Why?' question can become the new task from which to generate more 'How?' ideas (as illustrated in Figure A51.2):

TASK – To produce enough to meet orders

HOW? – Get more people to work machines *or* get faster machines

HOW? – Offer overtime *or* recruit more people

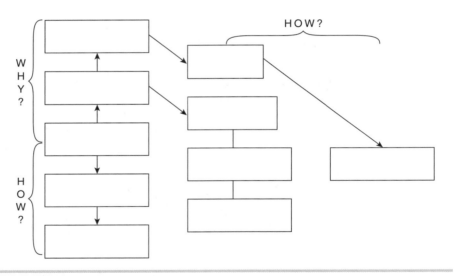

Figure A51.2 *'How' and 'why' activity*

The activity below offers you an opportunity to practise using both 'How?' and 'Why?' questions to analyse *activities* and *facts* relevant to your work.

Activity

Choose a current and problematic task or 'fact' connected to your work.

Write the task, activity or fact in the middle of a sheet of flipchart of paper and build your answers to the 'How?' and 'Why?' questions around it. It will look something like Figure A51.2.

In doing this activity, and in your thinking in general, you should aim to ask both 'How?' and 'Why?' questions and not just one or the other. This is the way to develop a helicopter mind, so that you can both hover above the problem *and* get right down to the details (or vice versa), and repeat this as often as you need to understand the situation truly.

Follow-up

You may find it useful to use some of your 'How'/'Why' analyses as the basis for discussion with others who share the same concerns.

If you want to go further and improve your IQ rather than just measure it, then you might enjoy Philip Carter and Ken Russell's *Increase Your Brainpower: Improve Your Creativity, Memory, Mental Agility and Intelligence* (Wiley, 2001). And if you really like that sort of thing, then the website for the 'intelligence' club, MENSA, is www.mensa.org.uk/mensa/global/resource.html.

On the other hand, the concept of IQ is increasingly challenged as rather narrow, as in Activity 48, *Your Multiple Intelligences*.

Daniel Goleman's influential *Emotional Intelligence* is amplified in many books and also numerous websites. See, for example, www.mindtools.com › Career Skills and www.businessballs.com/personal-development.htm. You can also take a 136-item test at www.myskillsprofile.com/tests/eiq16.

Managing Your Dependency

Managerial qualities	**Ability to learn**

The driving idea of this book is *self-development*, which holds that for real learning to occur you need to take personal responsibility for your own learning.

This means moving from:

■ *Dependence* – or accepting uncritically any instructions from teachers and other people with formal authority as the 'right way' to do things;
   to
■ *Independence* – or taking ideas from teachers and authority figures as suggestions which you may try out and evaluate for yourself, adding them to your repertoire of skills and practices if *you* judge them to work.

The *independence* philosophy can be overdone and lead to an obstinate unwillingness to accept any guidance from qualified people.

■ *Interdependence* – or *mature dependency* means making full use of the advice from people with genuine expertise and experience. In this way, wisdom is passed from person to person and generation to generation, so that we can benefit from others' past successes and failures and, in turn, pass on what we consider to be useful knowledge.

Activity

Step 1

Make a list of six or so major tasks or activities that you have to perform in your work: preparing budgets, negotiating and bargaining, designing new products or procedures, providing leadership for a team or group, advising others, selling things or ideas, planning operations, interviewing, and so on. Write them down in the first column of Table A52.1.

Table A52.1

Task/activity	Are you an expert?	Do you know an expert?	Do you believe an expert exists?	Or is it an, as yet, unsolved problem?

Step 2

Take each of these in turn, go through the questions below, stopping at the first one that you can answer 'yes' to. Put a tick in the appropriate column of Table A52.1 for each task or activity depending upon which of questions (a), (b), (c) or (d) you first answer 'yes' to. There should be only one tick in the table for each task or activity.

(a) In terms of the practical ability to carry out this task or activity, do you see yourself as expert, and that you can reliably deal with it?

(b) If no to (a), is there an expert or source of expertise that you know of who could provide you with help on this task?

(c) If no to (a) and (b), do you believe that somewhere an expert exists – a procedure, approach or person who can provide a reliable solution to carrying out the task?

(d) If no to (a), (b) and (c), is this then one of those tasks or problems for which no known solution exists at this time, and therefore that you have as good a chance as anyone else of finding one?

Step 3

Now treat each of your answers as a statement to be *tested*. Consider what *evidence* you have. Are you really fully competent? Can the 'expert' really produce results? Can you track down an expert or authoritative source of knowledge on the problem?

■ Consider whether your personality leads you to believe in, seek out and rely on experts, or whether you tend to go it alone. Does this help or hinder you?

It will be particularly useful if you show your conclusions to someone else who is familiar with the same tasks and problems, and who will give you an honest opinion about your conclusions.

■ Does your organization have a culture of relying on experts or of finding its own solutions? Does this work well or not?

Follow-up

You may find it useful to follow up this activity by exploring what expertise exists to deal with problems facing you. Try sources on the web, within your own organization, in libraries or in educational institutions in your area.

There are many self-development books on all aspects of this perennial topic. One way of scanning the field is via Vic Johnson's *Self Help Books: The 101 Best Personal Development Classics* (Laurenzana Press, 2012, Kindle edition).

Learning to Learn

Managerial qualities	**Ability to learn:** Self-knowledge: Sensitivity to events

There are five stages to learning a new skill or ability:

- Becoming aware of inadequacies in the way you do things and sensing a need for new behaviour.
- Identifying the behaviours involved in a new skill or activity.
- Practising these behaviours.
- Seeking and getting feedback on your performance.
- Integrating the behaviours into your repertoire of skills and abilities.

Lifelong learning is especially vital for managers and leaders because of their challenging and changing responsibilities. We used to believe that most human learning was done in the first five years of life; but more recently, we have become aware of the need and potential for continuing learning throughout life. Being able to learn from everyday experience is a skill in itself.

Learning to learn is therefore a new and vital activity for managers and leaders. This activity helps you to reflect on how you acquired your existing repertoire of skills and abilities, and to think about what you need to learn next and in the future.

Activity

Step 1

Think of two incidents in the past year when you were successful – 'high spots' or 'peak experiences' – the sort of thing you would talk about in a promotion interview to demonstrate your strengths.

Now describe these events – what actually happened and what did you do exactly? Write these down and be as *specific* as you can.

Event 1

What happened?

_____

_____

_____

What did you do?

_____

_____

_____

Event 2

What happened?

_____

_____

_____

What did you do?

_____

_____

_____

Step 2

From these two events, what were the key *skills abilities* or *qualities* that enabled you to do what you did and to achieve a successful outcome?

Table A53.1 Learning skills

Skill/ability/quality	Where did I learn it from?	How did I learn it?
1.		
2.		
3.		
4.		
5.		
6.		

Write these down in column 1 of Table A53.1. Then answer these two questions for each key skill, ability or quality:

(a) *Where* did I learn it from?
  - the boss?
  - school/college?
  - from doing the job?
  - a book?
  - from my colleagues?, etc.

It is also useful to recall over what period of time and at what stage in your life this skill/ability/quality was learned. Do this by remembering the latest time when you are sure you *did not* have the skill, ability or quality and the earliest time you *did*.

(b) How did I learn it, i.e. what process was involved? For example, by:
  - being told something?
  - imitating somebody?
  - puzzling it out for myself?
  - accident or on purpose?
  - through emotional or intellectual channels?, etc.

Step 3

From the data generated in Steps 1 and 2, write down the insights you have had so far about *how* you learn.

When you have noted as much as you can, reflect on the following questions about your learning processes. Write down any additional insights you get from answering these questions:

(a) Do the five processes of learning a new skill/ability/quality fit with your learning experiences or not?

_____

_____

_____

(b) Do you learn different things in different ways? If so, what things and in what ways?

_____

_____

_____

(c) Thinking about other people that you know well, are there any learning processes that they use which you do not?

_____

_____

_____

(d) Do you learn from receiving 'inputs' – being told or shown something?

_____

_____

_____

(e) Do you learn from imitating other people or by observing the success and failures of their actions?

_____

_____

_____

(f) What is the place of emotion and feelings in your learning? Is learning painful, pleasant or something else for you?

_____

_____

_____

Step 4

Find a friend, colleague or perhaps a trainer or facilitator and discuss your reflections with them. Working with other people in this way – sharing, listening, questioning, reflecting together – is a key learning process in adults and one you need to employ frequently if you are to become the lifelong learner *and* the manager and leader that you can truly be.

Learning how to learn is not easy and is, perhaps, the ultimate leadership and management skill. Understanding your learning processes is one way to improve your ability to learn. Work on this, and the rest of the managerial skills and abilities will come much more easily.

Follow-up

New approaches to learning include the use of Gardner's eight intelligences (see Activity 48, *Your Multiple Intelligences*) and a related field known as 'Accelerated Learning'. Most books on this are written for teachers rather than learners, but Brian Best's *Accelerated Learning Pocketbook* (Teachers' Pocketbooks, 2011) will give you a start. Guy Claxton's *Learning to Learn – the Fourth Generation: Making Sense of Personalised Learning* (TLO Ltd., 2006), though aimed at schools, is well written and thought-provoking because of its focus on learning and not on teaching.

The BBC offers lots of free on-line learning resources, many of which are very good. There are all sorts of personal development topics, for example, at http://www.bbc.co.uk/learning/subjects/personal_development.shtml.

Study Skills

Managerial qualities	**Ability to learn:** Professional knowledge and skills: Self-knowledge

We sometimes say 'she or he is very clever' of someone who is highly qualified, implying that they are more able than ourselves. Professional qualifications are often taken as a measure of a person's worth, and people of ability may nonetheless be handicapped by the lack of them. But basic ability is only one part of obtaining professional qualifications; opportunity and chance are often of equal significance.

Another critical aspect is application – sticking to the task – and this includes skills in studying. Study skills are different from some other components of academic success because you are not born with them and you do not acquire them by chance. You have to learn them.

Study skills are important whether you are professionally qualified or not. They are important to all leaders and managers because they contribute to that elusive skill of being able to learn from one's own experience (see Activity 53, *Learning to Learn*).

Start by looking at your own study skills. There is insufficient space here to become proficient in all these skills, but this activity will help you make a diagnosis and provide pointers for your next steps.

Activity

Step 1: Questionnaire 1 – study tasks

The *very best* way to use this questionnaire is to complete it *prior* to some period of study, and then after to see if you feel you have made an improvement.

To obtain an estimate of your existing level of study skills, complete Questionnaire 1 (Table A54.1) by circling 3, 2 or 1 for each of the 16 questions.

Table A54.1   Questionnaire 1 – study tasks

	This is a big problem for me	This is something of a problem for me	This is not a problem for me
For each question, circle one number – 1, 2 or 3 – in the columns on the right			
Here are some tasks which have to be achieved for successful study			
How difficult is it for you to ...			
1. ... decide on a suitable place for studying?	3	2	1
2. ... decide when to study, or for how long?	3	2	1
3. ... choose your goal (i.e. precisely what you want to learn)?	3	2	1
4. ... decide how to achieve your goal (i.e. what study activities to perform)?	3	2	1
5. ... obtain or reach people, books and other *resources?*	3	2	1
6. ... deal with lack of desire for achieving your goal, once set?	3	2	1
7. ... deal with dislike of activities necessary to reach your goal (e.g. you want to learn Spanish but you hate reading)?	3	2	1
8. ... cope with doubts about success?	3	2	1
9. ... estimate level of knowledge or skill – start and finish and also during study to determine progress?	3	2	1

(continued)

Table A54.1 (continued)

	This is a big problem for me	This is something of a problem for me	This is not a problem for me
10. ... deal with difficulty in understanding some part or through lack of fundamental knowledge at some stage?	3	2	1
11. ... be able to concentrate?	3	2	1
12. ... be able to remember?	3	2	1
13. ... be able to apply knowledge gained to real-life situations?	3	2	1
14. ... deal with frustration arising from speed to learning, material containing opinions rather than clear-cut 'facts'?	3	2	1
15. ... be able to overcome laziness or inertia despite interest?	3	2	1
16. ... find fellow learners for mutual stimulation and companionship?	3	2	1

Scoring

Add up the circled numbers.

The measurement that matters is one which matches you against yourself and not against some mythical standard. However ...

- If you scored less than 20, you have few study problems (at least as revealed by this questionnaire).
- If you scored between 20 and 30, you do have some difficulties. You need to do more work on your study skills.
- If you scored over 30, it is highly likely that your innate ability is being held back by inadequate study skills.

Step 2

Remembering that this questionnaire is only as valid as *you* think it is, go back through it and look at the questions where you circled 3. Then study the ones where you circled 2. Where are the difficulties?

For example, an inability to concentrate or to maintain motivation (both very common study problems) may be caused by a variety of things. There may be a very simple reason, such as working in a noisy or unsuitable environment;

or the subject you are trying to study may be exceedingly complex. Lack of concentration is a frequent result of emotional upset, and lack of motivation may stem from a deep-seated fear of failure, perhaps developed in childhood.

There are a wide variety of possible interpretations of your results. You might find it helpful to think through your results with a supportive person who can help you reflect.

Step 3: Solutions

Whatever your study difficulties, the good news is that there are answers, things that you can do to improve your skills. Depending on where the difficulties are located, here are some possible ways forward:

- Set yourself a STUDY DIARY, giving specific periods on given days of the week for study (Questions 2; 6; 7; 11; 15).
- Find a good PLACE for you to study (this may be combined with time) (Questions 1; 2; 5; 15; 16).
- Establish a SELF-TESTING procedure (Questions 6; 8; 9).
- Establish a rigorous PRACTICE ROUTINE (Questions 6; 7; 11; 12).
- Join a suitable study CLASS (Questions 4; 5; 9; 10; 15; 16).
- Consult an EXPERT or TUTOR (Questions 4; 5; 9; 10).
- Set yourself a detailed ACTION PLAN (Questions 3; 4; 5; 9).

And *especially*:

- Find a supportive FRIEND or ALLY – to talk to, to swap ideas, to counsel, to encourage, to discipline, etc. (all questions).

These are only some of the possible solutions (see Follow-up).

Step 4: Questionnaire 2 – study skills

So far we have considered overall study tasks – the problems to be overcome when studying usually alone and without a tutor. But there are also specific skills involved in studying, such as reading, writing, etc.

Now complete Questionnaire 2 (Table A54.2).

Scoring

Questionnaire 2 focuses on several key areas of study skills:

- organizing yourself and your time
- reading
- listening to talks or lectures
- note taking
- writing.

Table A54.2   Questionnaire 2 – study skills

	Rarely	Sometimes	Usually
For each question, circle one number – 1, 2 or 3 – in the columns on the right			
Here are some tasks which have to be achieved for successful study			
Do you . . .			
1. . . . decide in advance what you are going to study and *where?*	1	2	3
2. . . . set yourself goals and sub-goals (e.g. I will read this book between now and then; 30 pages here, etc.)?	1	2	3
3. . . . meet your deadlines – especially with regard to written work, reports, etc.?	1	2	3
4. . . . read fast enough to read all the books you need to read on any given matter?	1	2	3
5. . . . skim or scan through books using contents pages and indexes, before deciding what to read?	1	2	3
6. . . . consciously read for a purpose (i.e. to gain specific material and not just to 'get everything')?	1	2	3
7. . . . find it possible to concentrate when listening to lectures or talks?	1	2	3
8. . . . take notes when listening to talks or lectures?	1	2	3
9. . . . know how to use library systems to find the books or information you need?	1	2	3
10. . . . write key notes (i.e. headings and sub-headings rather than continuous prose)?	1	2	3
11. . . . feel at ease drawing up reports or writing papers?	1	2	3
12. . . . express yourself well in writing?	1	2	3

You should aim to be consistently circling 3s in this questionnaire.

Good study skills and habits take time and purposeful practice to master. You need to keep practising over time and with persistence until you have developed these useful habits. Good luck.

Follow-up

There are many books and resources on study skills. Search the web or consult your local training department, library or college and they will be certain to

have something to offer. The BBC and Open University are other good sources. See, for example, http://www.open.ac.uk/skillsforstudy/.

The Good Study Guide by Andrew Northedge (Open University/McGraw-Hill, 2005; Kindle edition, 2012) is a well-established and well-reviewed guide to ways of studying, essay writing and preparing for examinations.

Your Learning Cycle

Managerial qualities	**Ability to learn:** Self-knowledge: Sensitivity to events

Your Learning Cycle is founded upon the key learning experiences in your life. Together with Activity 53, *Learning to Learn*, and Activity 54, *Study Skills*, this activity will advance your learning abilities, which is a major goal of this book.

In adults, learning occurs when we become dissatisfied with our behaviour in the light of various experiences. If we are open and willing to learn, reflecting on our experiences can give us clues to new and more satisfying actions.

On the other hand, adults have so much accumulated experience that often this past experience gets in the way of the new: 'I have 10 years' experience of interviewing, I think I know most of what there is to know!'

Unexamined life events are not experiences – just things that happened. Experience is generated when we reflect. And this reflection can lead, often in small ways, to changed perceptions of situations and new ways in which we might act. This process or learning cycle looks like Figure A55.1.

Activity

Each of us is a unique blend of inherited characteristics modified over time by all sorts of experiences – some pleasant, some less so. And it is often these painful experiences that teach us the most.

In this activity you are invited to re-live some of these past experiences. What made them so important in making you the person you are today?

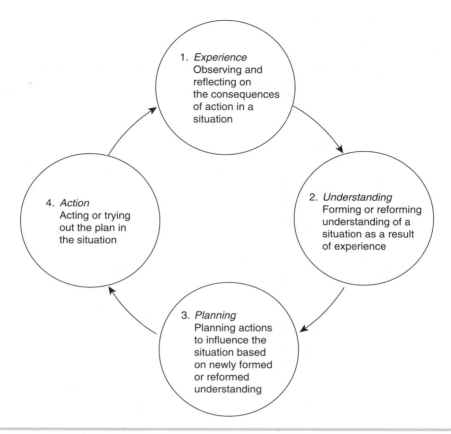

Figure 55.1   A learning cycle

Step 1

Think of the key learning experiences in your life – those that led to significant change in your long-term actions and behaviour.

Pick three, four or five of these key learning experiences. They may have been short or long in duration, but they must have resulted in a discernible change in the way you behaved. Label each with a title or phrase. Here are some examples:

- being punished
- going to school for the first time
- first love affair
- having a baby
- becoming able to work a personal computer
- broken leg
- university degree
- being praised.

Step 2

Take a piece of paper for each experience and label it. Divide the sheet into eight parts with horizontal lines and makes some notes in response to the following questions:

1. What happened?

   _____

   _____

   _____

2. What started it?

   _____

   _____

   _____

3. What did you learn?

   _____

   _____

   _____

4. What words describe how you felt while it was happening?

   _____

   _____

   _____

5. Who else was involved?

   _____

   _____

   _____

6.   Did they help or hinder your learning? How?

_____

_____

_____

7.   How would you describe the learning process?

_____

_____

_____

8.   What were the key characteristics of this event – compared with others in
     your life when you didn't learn as much?

_____

_____

_____

Step 3

When you have completed sheets for three, four or five key learning experiences, look back through them and seek out any connections and commonali-
ties there might be – in how things started; in how you felt; in who was involved,
etc. Can you see any patterns in your learning experiences?
   Note these down.

_____

_____

_____

_____

_____

Now look back through your learning experiences and make two lists – the factors that *helped* you to learn and those that *hindered* your learning:

Factors assisting learning	Factors hindering learning
(i)	(i)
(ii)	(ii)
(iii)	(iii)
(iv)	(iv)
(v)	(v)
(vi)	(vi)
etc.	etc.

Your key learning experiences are the source of the skills and abilities that you possess today. Understanding your learning cycle and patterns will help you get the best lessons from your future experiences as a manager and leader.

Follow-up

The books listed for Activity 53, *Learning to Learn*, and Activity 54, *Study Skills*, are also relevant here.

The learning cycle is found first in David Kolb's *Experiential Learning* (Prentice-Hall, 1985), which is a good book on how adults learn. Peter Honey and Alan Mumford have fashioned their *The Learning Styles Questionnaire, 80-item Version* (Peter Honey Publications, 2006) on Kolb's model.

Conversations with Yourself

Managerial qualities	**Self-knowledge:** Creativity

Talking to yourself – according to the playground joke – is a sign of madness. In art history, 'madness' and creativity are often closely linked and what was once described as lunacy would now be called non-conformity or even genius. It is often the abnormality in famous people, a deviation from some norm, which makes them outstanding. This is linked to psychologists' concepts such as divergent and convergent thinking or vertical and lateral thinking. It seems that a certain amount of experimentation and playfulness is necessary for creativity and learning.

This activity is simple, straightforward and powerful. You'll need a digital recorder, a private room and some uninterrupted time.

Activity

Step 1

Go into your room, lock the door, switch on the recorder and begin speaking to *yourself*. Do not address any audience or person, real or imaginary. Speak to yourself.

You may find this quite difficult or it may be quite natural to you. If you find it hard, you may need several starts before you get into it.

If you have any doubts, play back what you've said and check whether you are *really speaking to yourself*.

Step 2

When you have mastered talking to yourself, start on any specific problem or difficult situation facing you. Keep talking until you have said everything you wish to say about this situation.

Step 3

Play back the recording. Listen until you are satisfied that you understand yourself.

Step 4

Wipe the recording before leaving the room – whether you achieved Steps 2 and 3 in their entirety or not. *This is extremely important.*

Step 5

Repeat Steps 1–4 periodically as a means of getting in touch with the problem.

This activity is a formal way of thinking aloud – a more respectable occupation than talking to yourself. The theory is that whenever we speak, we speak to an audience. We always try to impress or achieve a specific effect upon another or others. We rarely, if ever, speak to ourselves to find out *what we really think*.

Creativity seems to be only partly a conscious process. There is only so much that can be done by the conscious mind. Often the 'aha!' or 'eureka!' experience comes after we have slept on or dropped a problem to think about something else. The assumption is that the unconscious mind worked somehow on the original situation and emerged with a solution or breakthrough.

Try it – you may break that block you've been struggling with for so long.

Follow-up

The books suggested in Activity 45, *Generating New Ideas*, and Activity 46, *Approaches to Creativity*, offer ways forward in developing your thinking and creativity.

Backwards Review

Self-knowledge: Sensitivity to events

The ancient dictum 'know thyself' is as applicable to today's leaders and managers as it was to the sages who coined it. To know myself – how I act and behave; what my strengths, weaknesses and learning needs are; what motivates and excites me; what scares and dismays me; the effects I have on others; and the effects different people have on me, are all important aspects of managing myself and leading others.

When we're going out, or to an important meeting, we may check out how we look – by glancing in the mirror. Knowing ourselves requires this sort of information, this reflection from some mirror. *Backwards review* is a reflective meditation that creates the mirror for ourselves. It is very simple and also quite profound. It takes practice to develop.

Activity

Step 1

This is a simple yet profound activity for becoming more aware of yourself and your situation. You can do it at any time, but it works well after any significant episode: after an argument, an important meeting, a momentous event, at the

end of a year. It takes practice to develop this skill, but it is a fundamental way of developing awareness and consciousness.

It is perhaps best done at the end of each day, just before you go to sleep.

Step 2

Find a quiet place to be and do the activity. You can do it sitting up, lying down, walking – whatever, as long it is a place for yourself free from interruption and distraction.

Step 3

Now begin to go through the events of the day (or meeting, week, month, etc.) in your mind:

Work *backwards*, starting with the most recent happenings.

- ■ Try to recall what happened in each event or episode – what did you do? What were you thinking at the time? What feelings did you experience?
- ■ What did you actually want to do at that time and what did you actually do?
- ■ What were other people doing and what were their thoughts, feelings and wishes?

(As you can see by now, this 'simple' exercise is quite a challenge. Do not give up.)

- ■ Try to picture, to visualize, what happened. Take each episode in turn going slowly backwards, bringing the picture of it into your mind.

(Some people find it easy to see pictures in their minds, others find it very hard.)

- ■ What did you do? What were others doing?
- ■ How did you feel? What were your thoughts? . . . and so on.

Step 4

Keep going as slowly as you like until you get to the end (actually the beginning) of the day (or meeting, week, etc.).

Don't be discouraged if you don't get this far and can only manage a few episodes or hours back. You could start just with an hour or so, and gradually extend the time.

If you work to develop this skill, you will become much more conscious of yourself, your actions, your thoughts and your feelings. You will also gain

insights into those of other people, and see more clearly what affects them and how their actions, thoughts and feelings affect you.

This reflective skill is one that you can use whenever you need it, especially perhaps when your mind feels dull or you need to be extra vigilant.

Follow-up

You can follow up this activity by taking lots of practice. MindTools has a page on reviewing at http://www.mindtools.com/pages/article/newISS_05.htm.

On reviewing for the purposes of improving action in a more organizational context, IFAD (The International Fund for Agricultural Development) has a good resource at http://www.ifad.org/evaluation/guide/8/8.htm.

PART 4

Trainer's Guide

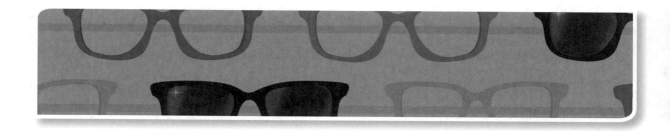

Trainer's Guide

Introduction

This book is written as an aid to self-development for managers, to encourage them to take the initiative and to enable them take charge of their own learning.

In this sixth edition, the book remains true to this aim, yet we know that many trainers and educators also use it in their work. Management and organizational developers use it for corporate leadership development activities, while tutors and educators use it on their post-experience and post-graduate programmes.

We have learned a lot from these colleagues about how the book can be used in these settings, and so this sixth edition contains, for the first time, this chapter – which addresses the facilitator or tutor rather than the individual manager or leader. There is no prescription here because each trainer, developer or educator will want to adapt and to use this book in the way that suits them best. However, here are some ideas and methods which have been fashioned by other people and which might serve as useful prompts to your own creativity and resourcefulness.

This short chapter contains some ideas for the developer when working with managers and leaders as individuals, in pairs, in small groups, classes and teams, and in terms of wider organizational learning.

Individuals

The book is designed for use by individuals working alone, but it can be used very effectively by any developer working one-to-one with clients or student managers and leaders.

Two of the most obvious possibilities are in Coaching or Appraisal situations where use of the diagnostic methods, followed by a careful selection of Activities, can lead a person to

discover things for themselves – which is a much more effective approach to learning than being told.

Here is a case example from a mentoring situation, where Sally, an energetic and effective worker on her own tasks, needs to develop new skills to be a good manager and colleague:

> *Usha, an external consultant, has been engaged to mentor Sally, a newly appointed team manager in a travel company. Sally has recently had her appraisal and received some feedback to the effect that whilst she is an outstanding performer in terms of completing her tasks and meeting her targets, she is seen as somewhat overbearing and insensitive to the needs of colleagues, including some of those in her own team.*
>
> *As a result of the conversation with Usha, Sally decided to go away and do three activities before their next meeting. She picked* Facts and Assumptions *on the grounds that she was sometimes too quick to make judgements about situations;* Credulous Listening *to develop her skills in this area; and* Getting to Yes *to practise a more collaborative style of negotiating. At the next meeting, Sally came back with some detailed Learning Journal entries about her experiences of working through these activities with different colleagues.*
>
> *Her reflections, and the insights that came in the subsequent conversations, made her realize that, if criticized in any way, she tended to be defensive, and attributed any fault to others or to outside circumstances. Identifying the issue that she wanted to work on for herself through the Questionnaire had enabled her to approach the Activities and the encounters with people with a more open mind. She had even asked a colleague for some help.*

Through using various Activities from the book, an individual manager or leader can be enabled to get some 'distance' on their actions and behaviour. As a result of this, in the case of Sally above, she was able to become less centred on herself and more able to see herself as experienced by others.

Many managers and leaders find themselves in situations where they are the responsible person, and are expected to act decisively on the basis of their own experience. Having the chance to discuss these situations with a coach or facilitator can be very enlightening, because these skilled professionals lead us to reflect on our own experiences, to draw our own conclusions, and to see that certain habitual courses of action are not inevitable but that there are other options.

Pairs

Where skilled coaches and facilitators are not available or are too expensive, the trainer or developer can tap the skills of their groups and classes and encourage them to practise their coaching skills with each other. These skills are not only a valuable asset to any manager or leader, but are becoming essential for generating good performance in the workplace.

But beyond these specific skills, the pair or twosome has a much deeper significance. As the fundamental unit in human society, it begins with that most profound learning partnership of mother and child. And for many of us humans, pairings of various kinds continue as the single most profound source of inspiration and satisfaction throughout life. The coach and coachee is a workplace expression of this fundamental unit, and even without the full professional skills, most adults can take on both these roles with one another.

Here are some examples of how pairs can be used to promote management and leadership development.

Pairings can be introduced into any learning situation. 'Sitting next to Nellie' is a tried and tested training technique that makes free use of the skills of the experienced to the benefit of the new starter. The idea of the 'buddy system' from the USA pairs up people to help each other, and in some schools, pupils in different years learn different things from each other, the older one often becoming aware of their helping capacities. So the pair, as the basic partnership, can be used anywhere and frequently in management development situations – from 5-minute exchanges in classes to much longer-term partnerships to generate learning opportunities for both partners.

Whenever there is more than one person using any of the Activities, people can always be paired for the whole or the part of this process. They can jointly choose an activity to take away, practise separately or together, discuss the findings and report back. Or, each person having completed an Activity, they can simply be asked to put their heads together for 5 or 10 minutes to share their findings and thoughts. Even a 2-minute exchange between temporary pairings can generate surprising results.

Pairings can also be used over the much longer term, as in this Open University programme:

In a post-graduate OU programme, diagnosis for personal development planning is part of the course. As part of this particular module, each student was asked to obtain a copy of A Manager's Guide to Self-development, and to complete the Activity Asserting Yourself and set some goals for self-development.

Once each person had completed this activity, they were paired together by the tutor based on who she thought had the most to learn from one another. Each person then shared the results of their analysis with a fellow student who questioned them about the specific examples given and which served as the basis for highlighting the priority areas for development. After each person had completed their turn, the pairs then contracted with each other to check progress on two objectives that they set to achieve over the life of the course.

In discussion, participants reported that being questioned about their concrete examples, in the areas that were highlighted for development, had made the assessment exercise very real and consequently that they had found it easier to set realistic goals to improve the situation.

So, never neglect the possibilities of pairings. The 'group of two' can be introduced into almost every setting usually and simply to generate variety and ideas and anywhere people are finding it hard. The Cornish tradition of 'Cousin Jack' – someone to help the newcomer get on their feet, and once found in every mining community in the world – comes from poverty-stricken miners forced to emigrate in search of work.

The development of coaching and helping skills through pairings is a beneficial byproduct of the activities described above. After reflecting on various learning assignments done in this way, people often comment on this learning and the insight gained in this process and almost incidentally.

Groups and classes

A *Manager's Guide to Self-development* is frequently used as the basis for workplace or classroom activity with groups of managers and leaders. It works particularly well with young or aspiring managers, and also with newly appointed leaders who may be very familiar with their work setting but who need now to look at it and themselves differently.

Here are three ways to use the book with groups and classes – group discussions, action learning sets and on-line forums. First, a way of deepening group discussions by enabling everyone to bring their experiences to the table.

Group discussion

The group discussion is a traditional recipe for working with groups but is surprisingly often squeezed out by input and presentations. It helps to avoid too much from the front by actually planning your discussion in some detail. The following format will take at least an hour to work through, not including the individual work in the first three steps:

- Choose an Activity(ies) to fit the needs of the group or syllabus, etc.
- Ask each person to go away to do the agreed Activity(ies) as an individual, in their own time and in their own environment.
- For the next session, ask everyone to bring back their experiences of carrying out the agreed Activity(ies) together with any data they have collected.
- After asking for general comments about these experiences, ask the class or group to divide into smaller groups of three, four or five to discuss their experiences.
- After an agreed time for small group discussion, ask each group to report back on their findings to the whole group.
- Discuss and list the main learning points.
- Allow time for each person to record his or her reflections in a Learning Diary.

A second approach to using the book with groups and classes demands even more from the participants than the willingness to engage in discussions.

Action learning sets

Action learning sets encourage people to change their actions and worlds and learn to be better managers from the process of doing this. Learning from attempting to change things is often much more profound than learning from lectures and discussions alone.

N.B. Working in an action learning way is only possible for people who are volunteers – so each person needs to choose for themselves to try this, and this choice needs to be an informed one – so you may need to explain the nature of action learning and something about the method before inviting people to take part and give it a go.

Follow the first three steps from the 'Group discussion' section above, and then:

■ Ask the group to divide into small action learning sets of four, five or six persons. Before the sets actually finish forming, make sure that everyone who wants to take part has a place in a set.

■ Now have each person in each set reflect on his or her personal experience and findings from the Activity chosen in the previous session. Ask each person to form a question from this experience.

N.B. The question should always start with 'How can I . . .?'

■ Now agree a period of time for the sets to work with the questions of their members. These questions and the discussions that arise should be confidential to that set, and not shared with other people without the consent of the person concerned.

The sets will work best if they follow these simple rules (to help with this, sets may elect a facilitator or chair or referee for each round):

○ Divide the time equally between the members.

○ Each person takes it in turn to put forward their question to the rest of the set: 'How can I . . .?'

○ For the first half of the time available, the other set members discipline themselves to stick strictly to asking questions and to avoid providing advice of any kind. The aim of this is to help the person to explore the issue and the situation where they are trying to do something.

○ In the second half of the time available, members should concentrate on seeking suitable options for action for the person concerned.

○ Finally, each person should end their turn by committing themselves to an action before the next session. N.B. This action may be quite small – for example, agreeing to talk to someone about the issue, or doing further research on the issue – but it must commit the person to taking action as a result of the discussion.

A final example recognizes that increasingly more education, training and development is delivered on-line. In these circumstances, participation by the group or students often goes out of the window and much on-line education is no more than simple instruction.

Enabling everyone to bring their experiences to the table and making them visible to all concerned requires a special effort and can utilize that most ancient of discussion areas – the forum.

On-line forums

A group of 12 students on an e-learning work-based learning module routinely shared ideas on their bulletin boards and forum spaces. Over time the tutor noticed that many of the topics raised resulted in conflict of one sort or another – with peers, with managers and with other sections or departments. The tutor asked the group to read the Activity Handling Conflicts *and announced a process for dealing with them. He would post one of the three cases up each week for the next three weeks. He asked the group to split into three, with four students agreeing to post an immediate first response to each case, a further four would comment on these responses and offer alternatives during the week, while the remaining four students would then try to 'tell a story from the other side'.*

At the end of each week, the first four students considered all the responses, alternatives and stories and posted those they preferred and explained why. The exercise was repeated in the second and third weeks with the three sub-groups rotating their roles so that everyone experienced all three modes of response. In the discussion following the end of the 3-week cycle, the general feeling was that the group was surprised, not so much by the variety of responses, but by their very different styles. One person reported that a fellow student's response was exactly what she would have expected from one of her peers in her actual conflict situation. By examining this response with the conflict styles and stories from the other side, she was able to develop a strategy for managing her own feelings about the conflict and for taking more appropriate action.

Teams

Teams are special sorts of groups that share common goals and within which the work of individuals is interlocked and mutually dependent. To get along together on a day-to-day basis, a lot of what is thought and experienced by individuals in teams goes unreported. Teambuilding events and away days can open up some of this data with a view to making the team operate more effectively and satisfactorily for all those concerned.

There are a number of ways in which *A Manager's Guide to Self-development* can be used in teams, many of which do not require a special teambuilding session. A simple way is to do an Activity together and share the results. For example:

■ Have all team members complete *The 11 Qualities of the Effective Manager* questionnaire.

■ Ask everyone to send in their results anonymously to a volunteer who will aggregate the results and produce a summary document on the strengths and development needs of the team.

■ Fix a time to meet together to discuss the results, including:

○ What strengths do we have as a team?

○ As a team, what should be our priority development needs?

○ How will we work together on what is missing from our team?

○ How do we avoid over-using our strengths?

○ Etc.

■ Agree an action plan for each person and a date to meet up again to monitor the above.

Working in this way will create a general team diagnosis as well as some actions for improvement.

There are all sorts of other possibilities for working with more specific qualities and issues which teams can fruitfully do together. In this example, a team of managers and teachers was responsible for a major change project in a large school:

As preparation for their first team meeting, the team leader suggested that each member look at the Activity: Practising Change *and complete the exercises for themselves, record their outcomes and observations in a diary. For the first hour of the first meeting, each person in the team shared what they had learned from their experiments, while the others asked questions about how these could be applied to their change project. Although some people took some persuading that this was a good use of time, there was a general agreement that this both opened people's eyes with respect to one another and also brought a freshness to the approach of the whole team.*

On the topic of organizational change, *A Manager's Guide* can be used in even more ambitious ways.

Activities with organizations and networks

Any question that is important to an individual manager or leader may also be of interest to their colleagues. While all the Activities reported here are all aimed at the individual, most can also be adapted and re-worded by the trainer or educator for use in the wider group, organization or network.

Take the Activity *Generating New Ideas*, for example, which is concerned with helping a person to develop their creativity. Managers can be encouraged, having thought about this on their own first, to check it out with their colleagues, perhaps via Linked-in or similar networks.

Step 5 of this Activity asks the manager to think of a real problem that they are currently facing, to write it down, and then to list all the likely ideas for resolving it that occur to them. The idea here is not to evaluate at this stage but to free up personal creativity and brainstorm the longest list possible. This can easily be changed to address a group of managers, a network or even a whole department or division of an organization.

For example, in answer to the e-mailed question, 'How could we become more innovative in our work?', a group of managers quickly produced the following list:

- benchmark others
- ask each other for help
- copy what our neighbours are doing
- study best practice in Europe
- help each other to take more risks
- risk sharing
- support colleagues who are trying new things
- question colleagues who keep doing the same things
- share every idea that works with each other
- talk more to each other about what we do and how we do it
- encourage people to move round more and change jobs, teams, etc.
- introduce job shadowing
- be much more experimental, trying new things out
- being less critical of each other
- being more critical of each other!
- practise appreciative enquiry on all issues
- encourage people to run with their ideas
- set up 'think-tanks' for key areas
- establish processes for gathering new ideas
- invite outsiders to ask questions about why we do things the way we do
- try a new management technique every month
- make sure that teams are made up of different sorts of people
- increase the diversity of people in the business
- build networking opportunities
- eat more fruit!

Generating this sort of list is a good start, and is perhaps the easy bit. But it does at least demonstrate a wider energy that might not be apparent without asking the question, 'Is creativity

just an issue for the individual or is it a cultural problem?' Perhaps from this start, a session can be organized at the next conference, or an item tabled at a policy discussion.

The book as a whole offers a very flexible design, and if you are working in a corporate setting you can use it at all stages of the development cycle: diagnosis, planning, implementation and evaluation. The early part is diagnostic, and the 360° option may be particularly useful here. If you have a competency model or the like in your organization, you can map these onto our *11 Qualities of the Effective Manager* and go from there through the various development stages. Evaluation, at least at the learning level, can be achieved by repeating the diagnostic so that you have a before and after comparison.